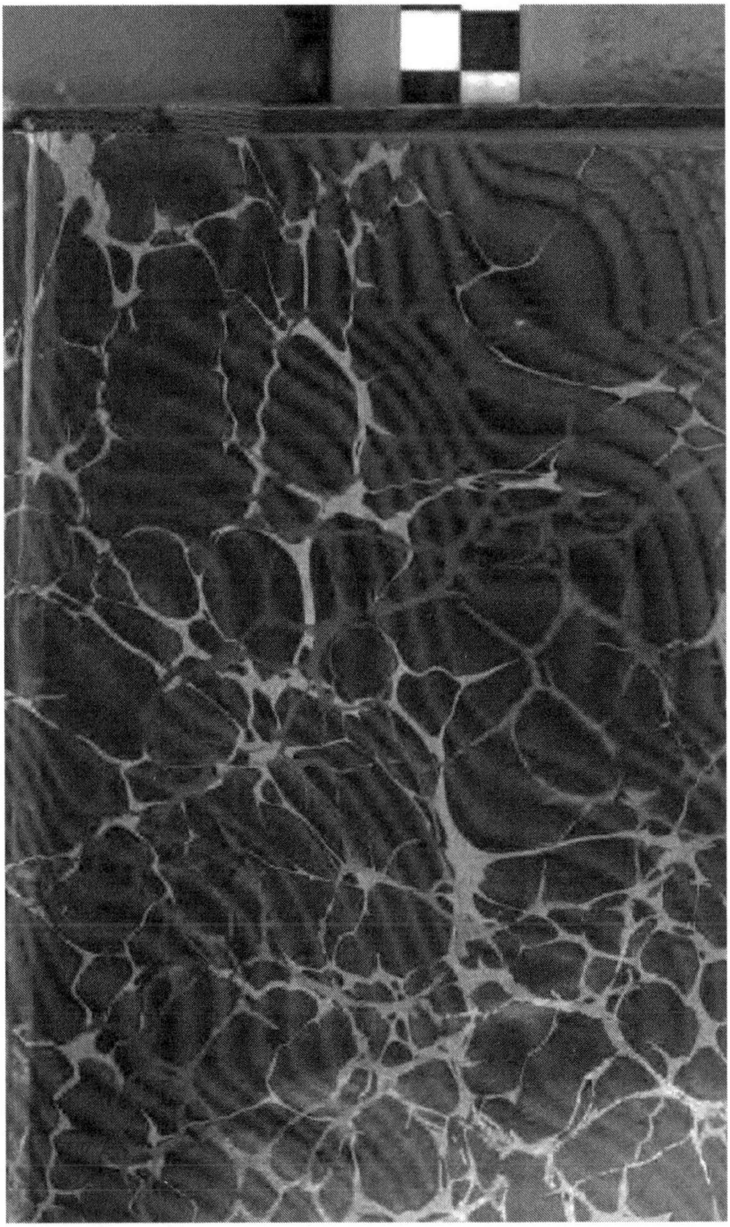

The

Italian Novelists

Volume One

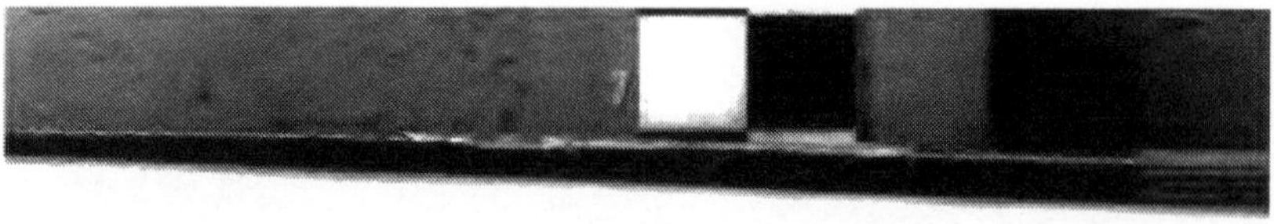

IMPORTANT ANNOUNCEMENT

The Society of Bibliophiles of London begs to announce to its members and those desirous of possessing copies of rare and choice editions, that it will publish a specially extra illustrated edition, limited to twenty-six lettered copies for the world, of which only ten copies are authorized for sale, of : : : : : : : : : :

The Italian Novelists

COMPRISING

The FACETIOUS NIGHTS of GIOVANNI FRANCESCO STRAPAROLA AND THE PECORONE OF SER GIOVANNI

NOW FOR THE FIRST TIME TRANSLATED INTO ENGLISH BY

W. G. WATERS

CHOICELY ILLUSTRATED WITH WATER-COLORS, PROOFS PRINTED IN TINTS, AND PROOFS ON JAPANESE PAPER.

FROM THE ORIGINALS BY

JULES GARNIER, of Paris, and E. R. HUGHES, A. R. W. C. S., London.

THIS EDITION IS LIMITED TO TWENTY-SIX COPIES, ONLY TEN COPIES OF WHICH ARE AUTHORIZED FOR SALE

IN SEVEN VOLUMES, PRINTED ON JAPANESE VELLUM PAPER ∴ ∴ ∴ ∴ ∴ ∴ ∴ AND APPROPRIATELY BOUND ∴ ∴ ∴ ∴ ∴ ∴ ∴

Price, Six Guineas (£6. 6. 0.), each volume

THE FACETIOUS NIGHTS OF GIOVANNI FRANCESCO STRAPAROLA consists of an exquisite and delightful collection of humorous, witty and mirthful conversations, fables and enigmas, including singing, music and dancing during the thirteen nights of the *Carnival at Venice*, as related by ten charming and accomplished damsels and several nobles, men of learning, illustrious and honorable gentlemen of note, at the entertainments of merriment and pleasure, given by the Princess Lucretia, at her beautiful palace at Murano, a suburb of Venice, and is now *for the first time translated* into English.

In the first twenty years of its existence "*The Facetious Nights*" was *sixteen times reprinted*, a figure which the "Decameron" reached only after a lapse of fifty years. Of the excellent French translation by Louveau and la Rivey, the first part of which appeared in 1560, *nine editions* were issued before the end of the century; an edition was produced at Amsterdam, and also in Germany, to which latter Dr. F. W. V. Schmidt affixed copious notes with the greatest care and learning. These notes, with those of the French and other editions, have been improved upon for this English translation.

The distinguishing feature of Straparola is *the great variety of subjects treated* in the fables. He is well known to every folk-lorist, seeing that he is regarded as *the principal* distributer of Oriental legends to the later fabulists and story-tellers of Northern and Western Europe.

One of the chief claims of "*The Facetious Nights*" on the consideration of later times lies in the fact that Straparola was the first writer who gathered together into one collection the stray fairy tales, for the most part brought from the East, which had been made known in the Italian cities—*and in Venice more especially*—by the mouth of the itinerant story-teller. He laid hold of whatever themes promised to suit his purpose best as a story-teller, careless as to whether other craftsmen had used them before or not, and these he set forth in the simplest manner possible. His aim was to lead his readers into *some enchanted garden* of fairyland; to thrill them with the woes and perils of his heroes and heroines; *to shake their sides with laughter* over the misadventures of some too amorous monk or lovesick cavalier. From beginning to end he certainly made free use of all the storehouses of materials which were available, selecting therefrom whatever subjects pleased him, and working them up to the best of his skill.

AS a masterpiece of Italian prose, "THE PECORONE" ranks next in celebrity to the "Decameron" amongst the collections of *Italian Novelle.*

Ser Giovanni was a contemporary of *Sacchetti*, and these two story-tellers come next to Boccaccio in order of time. The great popularity of "*The Pecorone*," which Giovanni in the Salutation and Proem claims to have written in 1378, arose from the fact that the stories of intrigue and adventure therein contained, covered comparatively fresh ground. All of Giovanni's stories were set forth with novelty, and were put on paper for the first time, to be borrowed from by certain of the better-known novelists and writers who followed him, amongst them being Shakespeare, for his character of "*Falstaff*," and his play of "*The Merchant of Venice*," which is founded on the First Novel of the Fourth Day. Quite a number of the stories treat of historical subjects, with *the salient in-*

cidents in the annals of his native Florence: the factions of Guelph and Ghibelline, and Bianchi and Neri. He likewise deals with certain events in the history of distant lands, Spain, France, England, Greece, Turkey, and the Tartars, and these, for the most part, are told with perversion of fact flagrant enough to be diverting.

The Royal Court Water-Color Edition

An especial feature of this edition is, that it is printed on Japanese vellum paper, and extra illustrated by a beautiful series of *hand-painted water-colors, proofs printed in tints, and proofs on Japanese paper.* It is strictly limited to twenty-six copies, *of which only ten copies are authorized for sale.* These will undoubtedly *increase in value* as the copies are subscribed for and become unobtainable.

only 10 sets [illegible] sold

THE

ITALIAN NOVELISTS

NOW FIRST TRANSLATED INTO
ENGLISH BY

W. G. WATERS

CHOICELY ILLUSTRATED BY
E. R. HUGHES, A.R.W.S., LONDON

IN SEVEN VOLUMES
VOLUME I.

LONDON: PRIVATELY PRINTED
FOR MEMBERS OF THE SOCIETY
OF BIBLIOPHILES: MDCCCCI

THE ROYAL COURT EDITION

With Text Printed on *Japanese Vellum* Paper

And Triplicate Set of Illustrations.

Aquarelles, Tints and Japanese Proofs

LIMITED TO

TWENTY-SIX COPIES

of which ten are authorized for sale

This is Copy

The Princess Lucretia And Her
Joyous Company Assembled
For The Entertainments.

Proem

The Princess Lucretia And Her
Joyous Company Assembled
For The Entertainments.

Proem

The Princess Lucretia And Her Joyous Company Assembled For The Entertainments

The Princess Lucretia And Her Joyous Company Assembled For The Entertainments.

Proem

THE

Facetious Nights

OF

STRAPAROLA

NOW FIRST TRANSLATED INTO ENGLISH BY

W. G. WATERS

CHOICELY ILLUSTRATED BY
JULES GARNIER
AND E. R. HUGHES, A.R.W.S.

IN FOUR VOLUMES
VOLUME I.

LONDON: PRIVATELY PRINTED
FOR MEMBERS OF THE SOCIETY
OF BIBLIOPHILES: MDCCCCI

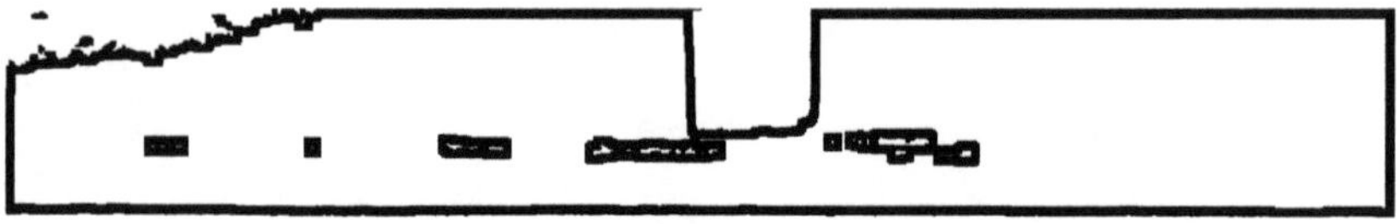

THE FACETIOUS NIGHTS OF GIOVANNI FRANCESCO STRAPAROLA

CONSISTS OF AN EXQUISITE AND DELIGHTFUL COLLECTION OF HUMOROUS WITTY AND MIRTHFUL CONVERSATIONS FABLES AND ENIGMAS INCLUDING SINGING MUSIC AND DANCING

DURING THE THIRTEEN NIGHTS OF THE CARNIVAL AT VENICE

AS RELATED BY TEN CHARMING AND ACCOMPLISHED DAMSELS AND SEVERAL NOBLES MEN OF LEARNING ILLUSTRIOUS AND HONORABLE GENTLEMEN OF NOTE AT THE ENTERTAINMENTS OF MERRIMENT AND PLEASURE

GIVEN BY THE PRINCESS LUCRETIA AT HER BEAUTIFUL PALACE AT MURANO

Dedication.

Greeting, To all gracious and lovesome ladies.

DEAR ladies, there are many envious and spiteful men who are always and everywhere attempting to fix their fearsome fangs in my flesh and to scatter my dismembered body on every side, contending that the diverting stories which I have written and collected in this volume are none of mine, but goods which I have feloniously taken from this man and that. Of a truth I confess they are not mine, and if I said otherwise I should lie, but nevertheless I have faithfully set them down according to the manner in which they were told by the ladies, nobles, learned men and gentlemen who gathered together for recreation. And if now I should let them see the light, it will not be for the sake of gratifying my own pride or to bring me honour or renown, but simply to please all of you, and especially those who may always count on my service, and to whom I owe continual devotion. Take then, dear ladies, with smiling faces the humble gift which your servant proffers, and heed not these snarling whelps, who in their currish fury would hang upon me with their ravenous teeth, but read my book now and then, taking such pleasure in it as time and place will allow, without, however, neglecting Him from whom comes all our weal. May you be happy, ever keeping in mind those who have your names graven on their hearts, amongst whom I do not count myself the least.

GIOVANNI FRANCESCO STRAPAROLA.

[This dedication in the edition of 1555 is dated from Venice, September 1st, 1553.]

A Foreword.

IT is somewhat strange that Giovanni Francesco Straparola, the author of "Piacevoli Notti," who in his own day was one of the most popular of the Italian novelists, should have been so long neglected. In the first twenty years of its existence the "Notti" was *sixteen times reprinted.* Of the excellent French translation by Louveau and la Rivey, the first part of which appeared in 1560, *nine editions* were issued before the end of the century. The distinguishing feature of Straparola is *the great variety of subjects treated* in the fables. He is well known to every folk-lorist, seeing that he is regarded as *the principal* distributor of Oriental legends to the

later fabulists and story-tellers of Northern and Western Europe.

One of the chief claims of the "Notti" on the consideration of later times lies in the fact that Straparola was the first writer who gathered together into one collection the stray fairy tales, for the most part brought from the East, which had been made known in the Italian cities — and in Venice more especially — by the mouth of the itinerant story-teller. These tales, incorporated in the "Notti" *with others of a widely different character,* were without doubt the principal source of the numerous French "Contes des Fées" published in the seventeenth and eighteenth centuries Perrault, Madame D'Aulnoy, and Gueulette took from them many of their best fables; and these, having spread in various forms, helped to tinge with a hue of Orientalism the popular tales of all countries — tales which had hitherto been largely the evolution of local myths and traditions.

Straparola turns towards *the cheerful side of things*, and the lives of the men and women he deals with seem to be less oppressed with the *tædium vitæ* than are the creatures of the Florentine and Sienese and Neapolitan novel-writers.

In the pictures he draws, Straparola illustrates life with a touch of pathos, as in the prologue to the second Night, *where he tells of the laughter of the blithe company*, ringing so loud and so hearty that it seemed to him as if the sound of their merriment yet lingered in his ears. There was, therefore, good reason why Straparola's imaginary exiles from the turbulent court of Milan should have sought at Murano, under the sheltering wings of St. Mark's Lion, that ease and gaiety which they would have looked for in vain at home; there were also reasons, equally valid, why he should make the genius of the place inspire, *with its jocund spirit*, the stories, with which the gentle company gathered around the Princess Lucretia wiled away the nights of carnival.

In the fables of adventure, and in every other case where such treatment is possible, Straparola deals largely with the supernatural. All the western versions, except Straparola's, of the story best known to us as "Gilletta of Narbonne" and as "All's Well that Ends Well," are worked out without calling in auxiliaries of any unearthly character.

The interest of the reader is kept alive, by accounts of the trials and dangers—a trifle ludicrous now and again—which heroes and heroines are called to undergo, the taste of the age preferring apparently this stimulant to *the intense dramatic power exhibited in the story of Malgherita,* and demanding that the ending should be a happy one, for the pair of lovers nearly always marry in the end, and live long and blissful years.

Proem.

The Princess Lucretia And Her Joyous Company Assembled For The Entertainments.

Proem

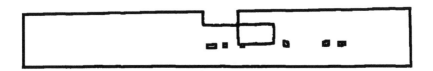

The Princess Lucretia And Her
Joyous Company Assembled
For The Entertainments.

Proem

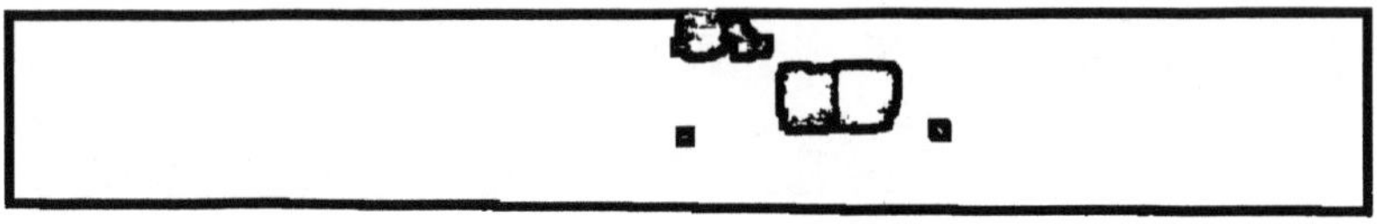

The Princess Lucretia And Her Joyous Company Assembled For The Entertainments.

Proem

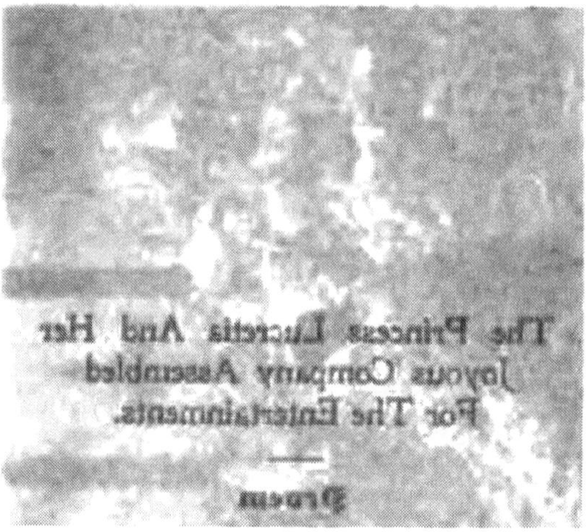
The Princess Lucretia And Her
Joyous Company Assembled
For The Entertainments.
Proem

Book the First.

PROEM.

IN Milan, the capital of Lombardy, an ancient city abounding in graceful ladies, adorned with sumptuous palaces, and rich in all those things which are fitted to so magnificent a town, there resided Ottaviano Maria Sforza, Bishop-elect of Lodi, to whom by claim of heredity (Francesco Sforza, Duke of Milan, being dead) the sovereignty of the state rightfully belonged. But through the falling in of evil times, through bitter hatreds, through bloody battles, and through the never-ending vicissitudes of state affairs, he departed thence and betook himself secretly to Lodi with his daughter Lucretia, the wife of Giovanni Francesco Gonzaga, cousin of Federico, Marquis of Mantua, and there they abode some months. Long time had not passed before his kinsmen discovered his whereabouts, and began forthwith to annoy him; so the unhappy prince, finding himself still the object of their ill will, took with him what jewels and money he had about him, and withdrew with his daughter, who was already a widow, to Venice, where they found friendly reception from Ferier Beltramo, a noble gentleman of most benevolent nature, amiable and graceful, who with great courtesy gave them pressing invitation to take up their abode in his own house. But to share the home of another generally begets restraint, so the duke, after mature deliberation, resolved to depart and to find elsewhere a dwelling of his own. Wherefore, embarking one day with his daughter in a small vessel, he went to Murano, and having come there his eyes fell upon a marvellously beautiful palace which at that time stood empty. He entered it, and having taken note of its lovely position, its lofty halls, its superb loggias, its pleasant gardens filled with smiling flowers and rich in all sorts of fruit and blooming herbs, he found them all highly to his taste. Then he mounted the marble staircase and surveyed the magnificent hall, the exquisite chambers, and the balcony built over the water, which commanded a view of the whole place. The princess, captivated by the charm of the pleasant spot, besought her father so strongly with soft and tender speeches, that he to please her fancy hired the palace for their home. Over this she rejoiced greatly, for morning and evening she would go upon the balcony to watch the scaly fish which swam about in numerous shoals through the clear salt water, and in seeing them dart about now here now there she took the greatest delight. And because she was now forsaken by the ladies who had formerly been about her court, she chose in their places ten others as beautiful as they were good; indeed, time would fail wherein to describe their virtues and their graces. Of these the first was Lodovica, who had lovely eyes sparkling like the brightest stars, and everyone who looked upon her could not but admire her greatly. The next was Vicenza, of excellent carriage, of fine figure, and of polished manners, whose lovely and delicate face shone with refreshing beauty upon all who beheld it. The third was Lionora, who, although by the natural fashion of her beauty she seemed somewhat haughty, was withal as kindly and courteous as any lady to be found in all the world. The fourth was Alteria, with lovely fair hair, who held her womanly devotion ever at the service of the Signora. The fifth was Lauretta, lovely in person, but somewhat disdainful, whose clear and languishing glances surely enslaved any lover who ventured to court them. The sixth was Eritrea, who, though she was small of stature, yielded to none of the others in beauty and grace, seeing that she had two brilliant eyes, sparkling even brighter than the sun's rays, a small mouth, and a rounded bosom, nor was there to be found in her anything at all which was not worthy of the highest praise. The seventh was Cateruzza, surnamed Brunetta, who, all graceful and amorous as she was, with her sweet and loving words entangled not only men in her snares, but could even have made descend from heaven the mighty Jove himself. The eighth was Arianna, who, though young in years, was grave and sedate in her seeming, gifted with a fluent tongue, and encompassed with divine virtues, worthy of the highest praise, which shone like the stars scattered about the heavens. The ninth was Isabella, a highly-gifted damsel, and one who, on account of her wit and skilful fence of tongue, commanded the admiration of the whole company. The last was Fiordiana, a prudent damsel, with a mind stored with worthy thoughts, and a hand ever prompt to virtuous deeds beyond any other lady in all the world. These ten charming damsels gave service to their Princess Lucretia both in a bevy and singly. The Signora, in addition to these, chose two matrons reverend of aspect, of noble blood, of mature age, and of sterling worth, to assist her with their wise counsels, the one to stand at her right hand and the other at her left. Of these one was the Signora Chiara, wife of Girolamo Guidiccione, a gentleman of Ferrara; and the other the Signora Veronica, the widow of Santo Orbat, of one of the oldest houses of Crema. To join this gentle and honourable company there came many nobles and men of learning, amongst whom were Casal Bolognese, a bishop, and likewise ambassador of the King of England, and the learned Pietro Bembo, knight of Rhodes and preacher to the citizens of Milan, a

man ot distinguished parts and standing highest in the Signora's favour. After these came Bernardo Capello, counted one of the chief poets of the time, the amiable Antonio Bembo, Benedetto Trivigiano, a man of jovial easy manners, and Antonio Molino, surnamed Burchiella, with his pretty wit, Ferier Beltramo, a courteous gentleman, and many others whom it would be tedious to name in turn. It was the custom of these, or at any rate of the greater part of them, to assemble every evening at the palace of the Signora Lucretia, and to entertain her with graceful dances, and playful discourse, and music and song, thus graciously beguiling the fleeting hours. Sometimes, too, certain problems would be propounded, to which the Signora alone could find solution; but as the days of Carnival drew nigh, days always vowed to playfulness and riot, the Signora bade them, under pain of her displeasure, to assemble next evening on purpose to arrange what manner of feast they themselves should keep. At the dusk of the next evening they all duly appeared in obedience to her behest, and, having seated themselves according to their rank, the Signora thus addressed them: "Honourable gentlemen and you gracious ladies, now that we are come together according to our wont, it seems well to me that we should order these pleasant and gentle diversions of ours so as to furnish us with some jovial pastime for the days of Carnival which are yet to run. Each one of you therefore will propose what may seem most acceptable, and the form of diversion which proves to be to the taste of the greatest number shall — if it be seemly and decorous — be adopted."

The ladies, and the gentlemen as well, declared with one voice that everything should be left to the Signora's decision; and she, when she perceived their will, turned towards the noble company and said: "Since it pleases you that I should settle the order of our entertainment, I, for my part, would counsel that every evening, as long as Carnival lasts, we should begin with a dance; then that five ladies should sing some song of their own choosing, and this finished, that these five ladies, in order to be determined by lot, should tell some story, ending with an enigma which we will solve, if our wit be sufficient therefor. At the end of the story-telling we will disperse to our homes for the night. But if these propositions of mine be not acceptable to you, I will readily bow to any other which may please you, and now I invite you to make your wishes known."

The project set forth by the Signora won the favour of all; wherefore she commanded a golden vase to be brought forthwith, and into this were cast papers bearing the names of five of the damsels present. The first to be drawn forth was that of the fair Lauretta, who, bashful as she was, blushed softly as the early hues of dawn. Next came the name of Alteria, then Cateruzza, then Eritrea, and then Arianna. The drawing over, the Signora caused to be brought in the musical instruments, and set on the head of Lauretta a wreath of laurel in token that she should make beginning of their entertainment on the evening following.

It now pleased the Signora that the company should fall to dancing, and almost before she had signified this wish to Signor Antonio Bembo, that gallant gentlemen took by the hand Fiordiana, with whom he was somewhat enamoured, and the others of the company followed this example straightway, and kept up the measure merrily. Loath to forego such pleasure, they gave over reluctantly, and bandying many soft speeches, the young men and the damsels withdrew to another apartment, in which were laid out tables with sweetmeats and rare wines, and there they spent a pleasant time in jesting one with another. When their merriment was over, they took leave of the Signora, who gracefully dismissed them all.

As soon as the company had come together the next evening in the beautiful palace of the Signora, she signed to the fair Lauretta to begin her singing, and Lauretta without waiting for farther command stood up, and, after respectfully saluting the Signora, went up on a raised platform, upon which was placed a beautiful chair covered with draperies of rich silk. Then having called her four chosen companions, they sang in tender angelic cadence the following song in praise of the Signora:

SONG.

Lady, by your kindly hand,
Which ever waits on love's behest;
By your voice of sweet command,
That bids us in your presence rest;
You hold in fee your servants' love,
And rank with spirits blest above.

You quit the city's din and heat,
And let us in your smile rejoice;
You call us willing to your feet,
To listen to our lady's voice;
Then let us loudly celebrate
Your dignity and queenly state.

And though upon our charmed sight
Earth's fairest visions soft may fall;
Your grace, your wit, your beauty bright,
Will blur them and outshine them all.
To laud another should we seek,
Our tongues your praise alone would speak.

When the five damsels gave over singing, in token that their song had come to an end, the instruments began to sound, and the graceful Lauretta, upon whom the lot had fallen to tell the first story of the evening, gave the following fable without waiting for further sign from the Signora.

Night the First.

Night the First.

THE FIRST FABLE.

Salardo, son of Rainaldo Scaglia, quits Genoa and goes to Montferrat, where he disobeys certain injunctions laid upon him by his father's testament, and is condemned to death therefor; but, being delivered, he returns to his own country.

IN every work, let it be good or bad, which we undertake, or propose to undertake, we ought first to consider the issue thereof. Wherefore, as we are now about to make beginning of our sportive and pleasant entertainment, I will protest that it would have been vastly more agreeable to me, had the lot willed it that some other lady should begin the story-telling; because I do not feel myself in any wise competent for the undertaking; because I am wanting in that fluency of speech which is so highly necessary in discourse of this kind, seeing that I have had scanter usage in the art of elocution than the charming ladies I see around me. But, since it pleases you, and has been decided by lot that I should be the first, I will begin — so as not to cause any inconvenience to this worshipful assemblage — my task of story-telling with the best of the faculties granted to me by divine providence. I will moreover leave open for those of my companions who shall come after me a wide and spacious field so that they may be able to relate their fables in an easier and more graceful style than I have at command.

Blessed, nay most blessed that son must be held to be who obeys his father with all due reverence, forasmuch as he thereby carries out the commands of the Eternal God, and lives long in the land, and prospers in all his works. And on the other hand he who is disobedient may be reckoned unhappy, nay most unhappy, seeing that all his undertakings come to a wretched and ill-starred end, as you will easily understand from the fable I am about to relate to you.

You must know then, gentle ladies, that at Genoa (a very ancient city, and as pleasant a one as there is in the world) there lived, not long ago, a gentleman named Rainaldo Scaglia, a man of great wealth, and endowed no less generously with wit and knowledge. He had a son called Salardo, whom he loved beyond all his other possessions, and this youth he had caused to be educated in every worthy and liberal art, letting him want nothing which might serve for his training and advancement. It happened that in his old age a heavy sickness came upon Rainaldo, who, seeing that his end was near, called for a notary, and made his will, which gave to Salardo all his goods. Beyond this he begged his son to honour his memory by keeping certain precepts ever in his mind, and never to act counter thereto. The first precept was that, no matter how great might be the love he had for his wife, he should never trust her with any important secret. The second was that he should never adopt another man's child as his own, supposing his marriage to be a fruitless one. The third was that he should never abide in a state, of which the chief magistrate wielded powers of life and death unchecked. Having given to his son these precepts, Rainaldo turned his face to the wall, and breathed his last.

After his father's death, Salardo, a young, rich, well-born gallant, grieved but moderately; and, in lieu of troubling about the administration of his estates or taking to heart his father's precepts, was in hot haste to find a wife, and began to search for one of sufficiently good descent, and with a person to his taste. Before his father had been a year dead, he married Theodora, the daughter of Messer Odescalco Doria, a Genoese noble of the first rank. She was very beautiful and of virtuous mind, though somewhat haughty, and Salardo was so deeply enamoured of her that he could not bear, night or day, to let her go out of his sight. For several years they lived together without a child being born to them; and then Salardo, yearning for an heir and disregarding the counsel of his father, determined to adopt a child and to bring him up as his heir. Having gained his wife's consent, he lost no time in carrying out his purpose, and adopted the son of a poor widow, calling the boy by the name of Postumius, and educating him with the utmost care.

In the course of time it happened that Salardo grew weary of Genoa, and determined to seek a home elsewhere, not because he did not find the city all that was fair and pleasant, but simply because he was infected with that desire for change which, not seldom, seizes upon those who live for pleasure alone. Therefore, with great store of money and jewels, and with sumptuous equipage, he left Genoa with Theodora his beloved wife, and his adopted son Postumius, and having traversed Piamonte, made a halt at Montferrat. Here he soon began to make the acquaintance of divers of the citizens, through going with them to the chase, and in other social gatherings in which he took great delight; and, in consequence of his wealth and generosity, he soon achieved a position of honour and repute.

The rumour of Salardo's splendid hospitality came before long to the ears of the ruling prince, the Marquis of Montferrat, who, when he saw that the newcomer was a handsome young man, well born, rich, of courtly manners, and ready for any gallant enterprise, took him into high favour and would seldom let a day pass without seeing him. At last, so great was the influence of Salardo over the marquis, it fell out that anyone who wanted a favour done to him by the latter would always manage to let his petition pass through Salardo's hands. Wherefore Salardo, mindful of the favour he enjoyed, was ever eager to devise some new pleasure for his patron, who, as became a young man, was much given to field sports, and kept a great number of falcons and hounds for the chase, and all appurtenances of venery, worthy of his high estate. But he would never go hunting or hawking save in the company of Salardo.

One day Salardo, being alone, began to consider the great fortune which had befallen him through the favour of the prince, and by-and-by his thoughts turned to his son Postumius, how discreet, and dutiful, and upright, and graceful he was. 'Ah!' he said to himself, 'my poor old father was indeed sorely in error about these precepts of his. He must, like many old men, have become imbecile with age; either this cause, or some frenzy, must have urged him to command me so particularly not to adopt a strange child as my own, or to become the subject of an absolute prince. I now see the folly of his precepts, for what son born to a father could be more sober, courteous, gentle, and obedient, than Postumius, whom I have adopted, and where should I find greater affection and more honourable treatment than is given to me by the marquis, an absolute prince and one knowing no superior? And, exalted as he is, he pays me so much worship and love that it seems sometimes as if I stood in the highest place, and he in one beneath me. Of a truth I know not what to think of it; of a truth it is a common trick of old people to forget the tastes and inclinations of their youth, and to lay down for their children rules and regulations, imposing thereby burdens which they themselves would not touch with the tips of their fingers. And this they do, moved not by love, but by the craving to keep their offspring longer in subjection. Now, because I have disburdened myself of two of the pledges imposed upon me by my father without any evil consequence, I will quickly get rid of the third; for I am assured that when I shall be free from it my dear wife will only love me the more. And she herself, whom I love more than the light of my eyes, will give ample proof of the imbecility, or even madness, of wretched old age, which finds its chief joy in imposing, with its dead hand, intolerable restrictions on the living. Truly my father must have been insane when he made his will, for to whom is my trust due if not to her who has left her home and kinsfolk and become of one heart and soul with me. Surely I may confide to her any secret, however important it may be; so I will put her fidelity to the test, not on my own account, for I doubt it not, but to prove her strength, and to give an example to those foolish ones who rate disobedience to the wishes of dead and gone dotards as an unpardonable sin.'

In these terms Salardo girded at his

father's wise injunctions, and deliberated how he might best rid himself of them entirely. After a little he left his house and went over to the mews at the palace, where the falcons of the marquis were kept, and of these he took one which was a great favourite of its owner, and secretly conveyed it to the house of a friend of his whose name was Francesco. He handed over the bird to his friend, and begged him, for the sake of the love there was between them, to hold it for him till the time should come when he might disclose the object of his request. Then, when he had returned to his home, he took a falcon of his own, and, having privily killed it, he bore it to his wife, saying: 'Theodora, my beloved wife, I, as you well know, find it hard to get a moment's rest on account of the many hours I am compelled to spend in attendance on the marquis, hunting, or fowling, or jousting, or in some other sport; and sometimes I hardly know whether I am dead or alive. Wherefore, to keep him from spending all his time over the chase, I have played him a trick he will relish but little. However, it may perhaps keep him at home, and give us and others some repose.' To this his wife said: 'And what have you done?' 'I have killed his best falcon,' Salardo replied, 'the favourite of all; and when he looks for it in vain I believe he will die of rage.' And here he lifted his cloak and took out the falcon which he had killed, and, having handed it over to his wife, directed her to have it cooked for supper. When Theodora heard this speech, and saw the dead falcon, she was deeply moved to grief, and, turning to Salardo, reproached him severely for his foolish jest. 'For what reason have you committed such a grave offence,' she said, 'and put such an insult on the marquis, who holds you so dear, and heaps such high favour upon you, and sets you above all others? Alas! Salardo, I fear our ruin is near. If, peradventure, the marquis should come to know what you have done, you would assuredly be in great danger of death.' Salardo answered: 'But how can he ever know this? The secret is yours and mine alone, and, by the love you have borne and still bear me, I pray you be careful not to reveal it, for if he should learn it our ruin would be complete.' 'Have no fear of this,' said Theodora, 'I would rather die than disclose it.'

The falcon was cooked and served at supper, and Salardo and his wife took their seats, but the lady refused to eat of the bird, though Salardo, with gentle words, enticed her thereto. At last, as she remained obstinate, he gave her such a buffet on the face that her cheek became scarlet from the blow. Wherefore she began to weep and lament bitterly that he should thus misuse her, and at last rose from the table, muttering beneath her breath that she would bear in mind that blow as long as she might live, and that in due time she would repay him. When morning was come, she stole early from her bed, and hastened to tell the marquis of the falcon's death, which news so fired him with rage that he ordered Salardo to be seized forthwith, and to be hanged without trial, and all his goods to be divided into three parts, of which one should be given to his wife as accuser, another to his son, and the remaining one to the man who should act as hangman.

Now Postumius, who was now a lusty well-grown youth, when he heard his father's doom and the disposition of his goods ordered by the marquis, ran quickly to Theodora and said to her: 'Mother, would it not be wiser for me to hang my father myself, thus gaining the third of his goods which would otherwise pass to a stranger.' And to this Theodora replied: 'Truly, my son, you speak well, for if you do this, your father's riches will remain with us intact.' So Postumius went straightway to the marquis to ask leave to hang his father, and thus earn the hangman's share, which boon the marquis graciously allowed.

Now Salardo had confided the whole of his secret to his faithful friend Francesco, and at the same time had begged him, when the hangman should be ready to do his work, to go to the marquis and beg him to let Salardo be brought before him, and graciously to listen to what he might have to say in his defence, and Francesco was loyal in carrying out this request. Meantime, the wretched Salardo, loaded with fetters, was awaiting in prison the hour which should see him led to a disgraceful death on the scaffold. 'Now I know,' he cried, with bitter weeping, 'that my good old father in his wisdom gave me those precepts for my profit. He gave me sage counsel, and I, senseless ribald as I am, cast it aside. He, mindful of my safety, warned me against my domestic enemies, and I have delivered myself into their hands, and handed over to them my riches to enjoy. He, well skilled in the disposition of despots, who in the space of an hour will love and hate, exalt and abase, counselled me to shun them ; but I, as if eager to sacrifice at once my substance, my honour, and my life, thrust my head into the jaws of this marquis, and put my faithless wife to the proof. Ah, Salardo, better had it been for you to follow in your father's footsteps, and let others seek the company of princes! Now I see into what strait my foolish confidence in myself, in my wife, in my wicked son, and, above all, in this ungrateful marquis, has led me. Now I see the value of the love of this prince for me. How could he deal more cruelly with me than by robbing me of my goods, my life, and my honour in one blow, showing thus how his love has turned to hate? I recognize now the truth of the proverb which says that a prince is like wine in a flagon, sweet in the morning and sour at eve. Where is now my nobility and my kinsmen? Is this the end of my loyalty, uprightness, and courtesy? O my father, I believe that, dead though you be, when you gaze into the mirror of eternal goodness, and see me about to be hanged, because, forsooth, I disbelieved and disregarded your wise and loving counsel, you will pray to God to have compassion on my youthful errors, and I, your disobedient and ungrateful son, pray to you also for pardon.'

While the unhappy Salardo was thus communing with himself, Postumius, with the air of a practised hangman, went with a body of police to the prison, and, arrogantly presenting himself to Salardo, spake thus: 'My father, forasmuch as you are bound to be hanged by the order of the marquis, and as the third part of your goods is to go to him who ties the noose, I am sure, for the love you bear me, you will not be wroth at the part I have chosen to play, seeing that thereby your goods, in lieu of passing to strangers, will remain with your own family.'

Salardo, after listening attentively to

this speech, replied: 'God bless you, my son; the course you have chosen pleases me much, and if at first the thought of death terrified me, I am now content to die after listening to your words. Do your office, therefore, quickly.' Postumius first implored his father's pardon, and then, having kissed him, put the halter about his neck, and exhorted him to meet death with patience. Salardo, when he saw the turn things were taking, stood astonished, and, after a little, was led out of prison with his arms bound and a halter round his neck, and, accompanied by the hangman and the officers, was hurried towards the place of execution. Arrived there, he turned his back towards the ladder which stood against the gibbet, and in this attitude he mounted step by step. When he had reached the top he looked down courageously upon the assembly, and told them at full length the cause which had brought him there, and with gentle words he implored pardon for any affront he might have given, and exhorted all young people to be obedient to their fathers. When the people heard for what cause Salardo was condemned, there was not one who did not lament his unhappy fate and pray he might yet be pardoned.

While the events above named were taking place, Francesco betook himself to the palace, and, having been introduced, thus addressed the marquis: 'Most worshipful sir, if ever you have been prompted to show pity towards anyone, you are now doubly bound to deal mercifully with the case of this friend of yours who is now, for no fault of his, led out to suffer a shameful death. Consider, my lord, for what reason you condemned Salardo, who loved you so dearly, and never by thought or deed wrought an offence against you. Most gracious prince, only suffer your faithful friend to be brought into your presence, and I will clearly demonstrate to you his innocence.' The marquis, with his eyes aflame with rage at Francesco's petition, made an effort to thrust him out of his presence, but the suppliant threw himself down at the feet of the marquis, and, embracing his knees, cried out with tears: 'As you are a just prince, have pity, O noble marquis! and let not the guiltless Salardo die because of your anger. Calm yourself, and I will prove his innocence; stay your hand but one hour, for the sake of that justice which you and your fathers have always reverenced, lest it be said of you that you put your friend to death without cause.'

The marquis, violently angered against Francesco, now broke silence: 'I see you wish to go the way of Salardo. If you go on enraging me thus I will assuredly have you set by his side.' 'My lord,' Francesco replied, 'I ask for no greater boon than to be hanged alongside Salardo, if, after having made inquiry, you do not find him innocent.' This last speech moved the marquis somewhat, for he reasoned that Francesco would never have spoken thus without being assured of Salardo's innocence, seeing that he thereby ran the risk of the halter himself. Wherefore he accorded the hour's delay, and, having warned Francesco that he must look to be hanged if he should fail to prove his friend's innocence, he sent a messenger straightway to the place of justice with an order to delay the execution, and to bring Salardo, bound as he was and with the rope about his neck, and the hangman and officers as well, into his presence without delay.

Salardo, on being brought before the marquis, noted that his face was still clouded with anger, and outspake at once with clear voice and undaunted carriage: 'My lord, the service I freely gave you, and the love I bore you, scarcely deserved such a reward as the shame and indignity you have put upon me in thus condemning me to a disgraceful death. I admit that my folly, so to call it, deserved your anger; but I was guilty of no crime heinous enough to warrant you in condemning me thus hastily and unheard. The falcon, on account of which your anger was kindled, lives safe and sound. It was never in my mind to kill it or to insult you. I wanted to use it as a means of trying an experiment, the nature of which I will now disclose to you.' Having thus spoken, Salardo bade Francesco go fetch the falcon and return it to its master; and then he told the marquis the whole story of the precepts he had received from his father, and how he had disregarded every one. The marquis, when he listened to this frank and candid speech, and saw his falcon, handsome and well nourished as ever, was, for the moment, struck dumb; but when he had fully realized his error of having condemned a guiltless man to death unheard, he raised his eyes, which were full of tears, and turned them on Salardo, saying: "Salardo, if you could clearly realize all I feel at this moment, you would know that the pain you have suffered from the halter round your neck and the bonds about your arms is as nought compared with the anguish which now torments me. I can hardly hope ever to be happy again after having done so grievous an injury to you, who loved and served me so faithfully. If it were possible that all should be undone, how gladly would I undo it; but, since this is out of the question, I will do my utmost to wipe out my offence, and to give you all the reparation I can.'

Having thus spoken, the marquis with his own hands unfastened the halter from Salardo's neck, and loosened his bonds, embracing him the while with the greatest tenderness; and, having taken him by the right hand and led him to a seat by his own, he ordered the halter to be put round the neck of Postumius, and the youth to be led away to execution, because of his wicked conduct; but this Salardo would not permit. 'Postumius,' he said to the wretched youth, 'what shall I now do with you, whom, for the love of God, I have nurtured from childhood, only to be so cruelly deceived? On one side is my past love for you; on the other, the contempt I feel for the wicked deed you planned to do. One calls upon my fatherly kindness to forgive you, the other bids me harden my heart against you. What then shall I do? If I pardon you, men will jeer at my weakness; if I punish you as you deserve, I shall go counter to the divine exhortation to forgiveness. But that men may not tax me either with too great leniency, or too great severity, I will neither make you suffer in your person, nor will I myself endure the sight of you any more; and in place of my wealth which you so greedily desired, you shall have the halter which you knotted round my neck, and keep it always as a remembrance of your wicked deed. Now begone, and let me never see you or hear of you again.'

With these words he drove out the wretched Postumius, of whom nothing more was ever heard. Theodora, as soon as she was told of Salardo's liberation, fled to a certain convent, where she soon ended her days miserably, and Salardo, when he heard the news of her death, took leave of the marquis and returned to Genoa, where, after having given away all the wealth he did not want for his own use, he lived long and happily.

During the telling of Lauretta's story divers of the hearers were moved to tears, but when they heard that Salardo had been delivered from the gibbet, and Postumius ignominiously expelled, and of Theodora's flight and ill-starred end, they were heartily glad. The Signora gave the word to Lauretta to propound her enigma, so that the order of entertainment agreed upon the previous evening might be observed, and the damsel with a smiling face gave it in these words:

In a prison pent forlorn,
A tiny son to me was born.
Ah, cruel fate! The savage elf,
Scarce bigger than a mite himself,
Devoured me in his ravenous lust,
And changed me into sordid dust.
A mother fond I was of late,
Now worse e'en than a slave's my fate.

The fair Lauretta, when she saw that no one was likely to solve her riddle, said, "This enigma of mine concerns the dry bean which is imprisoned between two husks; where, later on, she engenders a worm no bigger than a mite. This worm feeds upon her, and finally consumes her, so that not only is she destroyed as a mother, but not even the condition of a servant is possible for her." All were pleased at Lauretta's explanation, and Alteria, who sat next to her, having been selected as the next speaker, began at once her story without awaiting the Signora's command.

THE SECOND FABLE.

Cassandrino, a noted robber, and a friend of the prætor of Perugia, steals the prætor's bed and his horse Liardo, but afterwards becomes a man of probity and good repute.

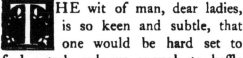

THE wit of man, dear ladies, is so keen and subtle, that one would be hard set to find a task arduous enough to baffle it. There is, indeed, a familiar saying of the common people, that a man does what he wishes to do; and this same proverb it is which has suggested to me the tale I am about to tell you. Although it is somewhat ridiculous, it may yield you some pleasure, or even instruction, by demonstrating to you the cunning of those who are thieves by profession.

In Perugia, an ancient and noble city of Romagna, renowned for its learning and for sumptuous living, there abode, not very long ago, a handsome young scapegrace named Cassandrino. So ill was his reputation with the citizens, on account of his many robberies, that frequent and lengthy complaints thereanent were made to the prætor by men of all stations in the city; but this latter, though he rated Cassandrino soundly for his misdeeds, seemed loath to punish him. Now, though Cassandrino was, past gainsaying, a thievish knave, he had one virtue which at least got him credit with the prætor, that is, he did not rob for the mere love of pelf so much as to be able, now and then, to spend magnificently and to offer handsome gifts to those who favoured him. Wherefore, and because he was affable, courteous, and witty, the prætor looked upon him so kindly that he would rarely let pass a day without seeing him.

But since Cassandrino persisted in these more or less reprehensible courses, the prætor was forced to give ear to the complaints which, with full justice, were laid against him. Being still reluctant to bring the culprit to justice, on account of the kindly feeling in his heart, he summoned Cassandrino one day into an inner chamber, and began to admonish him with friendly words, and to exhort him to have done with his evil ways, warning him of the perils he was risking thereby. Cassandrino listened attentively to the prætor's words, and spake thus in reply: 'Sir, I hear and clearly understand the good counsel which you, of your great courtesy, have given to me, and I know full well that it springs from the generous affection in which you hold me, and for which I am most grateful. I am indeed grieved that we should be plagued with certain foolish people jealous of others' well-being, and ever ready to blast their honour with spiteful words. These busybodies, who bear such tales about me, would do better to keep their venomous tongues between their teeth than to let them run on to my hurt.' The prætor, swayed by his affection for the speaker, needed very little persuasion to believe Cassandrino's story and to turn a deaf ear to the plaints of his ravages made by the citizens. It chanced soon after that Cassandrino, being a guest at the prætor's table, told him of a youth who was so marvellously light-fingered that he could steal anything he had a mind to, however carefully guarded and protected it might be. The prætor, when he heard this, laughed and said:

'Cassandrino, this youth can be no other than you yourself, for there cannot be another such a crafty trickster; but, to put you to the test, I will promise you a hundred golden florins if you succeed to-night in stealing the bed out of the chamber in which I sleep.' Cassandrino seemed somewhat disturbed at these words, and then answered: 'Sir, you evidently take me for a thief; but let me tell you I am not one, nor the son of one. I live by the sweat of my brow, and by my own industry, such as it is, and do for myself the best I can. But if it be your will to bring me to the gallows on this score, I will go there gladly for the sake of the regard I have ever had, and still have, for you.' After this speech Cassandrino withdrew, for he was very anxious to humour the prætor's whim, and he went about all day cudgelling his brains to devise how he might steal the prætor's bed from under him without betraying himself. At last he hit on the following scheme.

A certain doctor of the city had lately died, and on that very day had been buried in his family vault. After midnight Cassandrino stole to the burying-place, and, having opened the vault, drew therefrom the dead body of the doctor by the feet, and, after he had stripped it, dressed it again in his own clothes, which fitted so well that any one would have taken it for Cassandrino and not for the doctor. He hoisted the corpse upon his shoulders as well as he could, and, having made his way safely to the palace, he scaled the roof, with the doctor's body on his back, by a ladder which he had provided, and began noiselessly to remove the tiles with an iron crowbar, finally making a large hole in the ceiling of the room in which the prætor was sleeping.

The prætor, who was wide awake, heard distinctly all that was going on, and laughed to himself, though his roof was being pulled to pieces, for he expected every moment to see Cassandrino enter the room and attempt to carry off the bed. 'Ah! Messer Cassandrino,' he said to himself, 'you will not steal my bed to-night.' But while he was thus chuckling and expecting the attempt, Cassandrino let fall the dead body of the doctor through the breach in the ceiling into the prætor's room. The noise it made caused him to jump out of bed and light a candle, and then he saw what he took to be the body of Cassandrino (because it was dressed in that worthy's clothes) lying mangled and huddled together on the floor. When he recognized the garments, he was profoundly grieved, and cried out, 'Ah, what a wretched sight is here! To gratify my silly caprice I have killed this man. What will men say if it be noised abroad that he met his end in my house? Of a truth one needs to be careful.' The prætor, lamenting thus, went to rouse a faithful servant of his, and having awakened him, told him of the unhappy mischance, and begged him go dig a hole in the garden and bury therein the dead body, so as to prevent scandal. Whilst the prætor and his servant were burying the dead body in the garden, Cassandrino, who had silently watched the prætor's movements, as soon as the coast was clear let himself down by a rope, and having made a parcel of the bed, carried it away with all possible haste. After he had buried the body, the prætor returned to his room; but when he prepared to get into bed, no bed was there. He slept little that night, wherefore he had plenty of time to ponder over the cunning and dexterity of his friend Cassandrino.

The next day Cassandrino, according to his wont, went to the palace and presented himself to the prætor, who, as soon as he had set eyes on him, said: 'In truth, Cassandrino, you are the very prince of thieves! who else would have contrived so cunningly to steal my bed?' Cassandrino was silent, feigning the utmost astonishment, as if he had had no part in the affair. 'You have played an excellent trick upon me,' the prætor went on to say, 'but I must get you to play me yet another, in order that I may judge how far your ingenuity can carry you. If you can manage to-night to steal my horse, Liardo — the best I ever had — I will give you another hundred florins, in addition to the hundred I have already promised you.' Cassandrino, when he heard of this fresh task which was put upon him, feigned to be much troubled, and loudly lamented that the prætor should hold him in such ill repute, begging him at the same time not to be his ruin. The prætor, deeming that Cassandrino refused assent to his request, grew angry and said, 'Well, if you will not do as I bid you, look for no other fate than to hang by a halter from the city wall.' Cassandrino, who now saw that his case was dangerous, and in no small measure,[1] replied: 'I will do all I can to gratify you in what you ask, but

[1] Orig., *ed importar altro, che finocchi.*

believe me the task you propose is one beyond my power;' and with these words he departed.

As soon as he was gone, the prætor, who was resolved this time to put Cassandrino's ingenuity to no light trial, called one of his servants and thus addressed him: 'Go to the stable, and saddle and bridle my horse Liardo; then mount him, and keep all night on his back, taking good heed the while that he be not stolen.' And he gave orders to another to see that all the doors of the palace were well secured with bolts. That night Cassandrino took all his implements, and repaired to the principal gate of the palace, where he found the porter quietly dozing; but, because he knew well all the secret issues of the place, he let the porter sleep on, and, making use of another passage, he gained the courtyard, and thence passed on to the stables, which he found fast locked. With very little trouble he unfastened the door, and having opened this, he perceived, to his amazement, that a man was sitting on the prætor's favourite horse, with the reins in his hand, but when he approached he saw the fellow was sound asleep. The crafty rascal, noting that the sleeping varlet was senseless as a statue, at once hit upon a plan, clever beyond belief. He carefully measured the height of the horse, and then stole away into the garden, from whence he brought back four stout poles, such as are used in supporting vines on a trellis; and having sharpened them at the ends, he cunningly cut the reins, which the sleeping servant held in his hand, and the breast-strap, and the girths, and the crupper, and every other bond which stood in his way. Then, having fixed one of the poles in the ground, with the upper end dexterously inserted under one corner of the saddle, he did exactly the same on the other side, and repeated the operation at the other two remaining corners. Next he raised the saddle off the horse's back (the servant being sound asleep all the while), and let it rest entirely on the four poles which were firmly fixed in the ground. Then, there being no obstacle in his way, he haltered the horse, and led it off.

The prætor was astir early the next morning, and repaired forthwith to the stable, where he expected to find his horse all safe; but the sight which met his eyes was his servant, still sitting fast asleep on the saddle propped up by four poles. The prætor, having awakened him, loaded him with abuse, and, half dazed with what he had seen, quitted the stable and returned to the palace. At the usual hour in the morning Cassandrino betook himself to the palace, and gave the prætor a merry salute when he appeared. 'Cassandrino,' said the latter, 'assuredly you carry off the palm amongst thieves. I may indeed dub you with the title of "King of the thieves," but still should like to ascertain whether you are a man of wit and cleverness. You know, I think, Messer Severino, the priest of Sangallo, a village hard by. Well, if you bring him here to me tied up in a sack, I promise to give you as much money again as you have already earned; but if you fail in this, be sure that I will hang you up by the neck.' This Messer Severino was a man of holy life, and of the best repute, but in no wise experienced in worldly affairs, seeing that he cared for nought else but the service of his church. Cassandrino, perceiving that the prætor had set his mind on working him an injury, said to himself: 'This man, I plainly see, is bent on doing me to death; but in this he will find himself mistaken, for I will execute this task if it is to be done.' Cassandrino, being thus anxious to do the prætor's bidding, cast about how he might play a trick upon the priest which would serve the purpose he had in view, and ultimately fixed on the following stratagem. He borrowed from a friend of his a priest's alb, long enough to come down to his heels, and a well-broidered stole, and these he took home to his lodging. Then he got ready a pair of beautiful wings, painted in divers colours, which he had fashioned out of pasteboards, and also a diadem of tinsel, which shone radiantly. At nightfall he stole out of the town with his gewgaws, and went towards the village where Messer Severino abode, and there he hid himself in a thicket of sharp thorns, and lay close till the day began to dawn. Then Cassandrino put on the alb, and the stole round about his neck, and set the diadem on his head, and fixed the wings on his shoulders. Having done this, he hid himself again, and stirred not till the time had come when the priest should go forth to ring the bell for the Ave Maria. Scarcely had Cassandrino vested himself, when Messer Severino, with his acolyte, arrived at the church door, which he left open, and went in to do his morning office. Cassandrino, who was on the watch, saw that the door of the church was standing open while the good priest was ringing the bell, crept out of his hiding-place, stole softly into the church, and, when he had entered, went up to the altar and stood upright, holding open a large sack in his hands. Next he cried out in a low chanting voice: 'Whoever wishes to enter into the joys of paradise, let him get into this sack;' and these words he repeated over and over again. While he was performing this mummery, the acolyte came out of the sacristy, and, when he saw the snow-white alb, and the diadem shining brilliant as the sun, and the wings as gorgeous as a peacock's — to say nothing of the words he heard — he was altogether amazed; but when he had somewhat recovered, he went off to find the priest, and said to him: 'Sir, sir, I have just seen in the church an angel of heaven, holding a sack in his hands, who said: "Whoever wishes to enter into the joys of paradise, let him get into this sack;" and I, for my part, have made up my mind to do as he bids me.'

The priest, who was not over well-furnished in the upper storey, gave full credence to the acolyte's tale, and, as soon as he had issued from the sacristy, saw the angel standing there, clad in celestial garb, as the acolyte had said. Now Messer Severino was powerfully moved by the angel's words, and being mightily anxious to get safe to paradise, and at the same time somewhat in fear lest the clerk should forestall him by getting first into the sack, made believe to have left his breviary behind him at his lodging, and said to the acolyte: 'Go quickly home and search my chamber diligently, and bring back my breviary which I have left somewhere.'

And while the acolyte was gone to search for the breviary the priest approached the angel, making the while a deep reverence, and crept into the sack. Cassandrino, who was full of sharp cunning and mischief, seeing that the game was going as he wished, closed the sack's mouth at once and tied it firmly. Then he took off the alb, the diadem, and the wings, and having made a bundle of these and hoisted it, together with the sack, on his shoulders, he set out for Perugia, where he arrived as soon as it was clear daylight, and at the accustomed hour presented himself before the prætor with the sack on his back. Having untied the mouth, he lugged out Messer Severino, who, finding himself in the presence of the prætor, and more dead than alive—conscious likewise that a fool's trick had been played with him—made a weighty charge against Cassandrino, crying out at the top of his voice that he had been robbed and inveigled by craft into the sack, to his great loss and humiliation, and begging the prætor to make an example of him, nor to let so great a crime go without severe punishment, so as to give a clear warning to all other malefactors. The prætor, who had already fathomed the business from beginning to end, could not contain his laughter, and turning to

Messer Severino thus addressed him: 'My good father and my friend, say not another word and do not distress yourself, for you shall never want any favour, nor fail to have justice done to you; although, as I see quite clearly, you have just been made the victim of a joke.' The prætor had to say and do his best to pacify the good priest, and, having taken a little packet wherein were several pieces of gold, he gave it to him and directed that he should be escorted out of the town. Then, turning to Cassandrino, he said to him: 'Cassandrino, Cassandrino, of a truth your knavish deeds outdo your knavish reputation which is spread abroad. Wherefore, take these four hundred golden florins which I promised you, because you have fairly gained them, but take care that you bear yourself more decently in the future than you have borne yourself in the past, for if I hear any more complaints of your knavish pranks, you shall certainly be hanged.'

Cassandrino hereupon took the four hundred golden florins, and having duly thanked the prætor for them, went his way, and with this money he traded skilfully and successfully, and in time became a man of business highly respected by all.

The ladies and gentlemen were much pleased with Alteria's story, and she being called upon by the Signora gave her enigma in the following terms:

> While I my nightly vigil kept,
> A man I spied, who softly crept
> Adown the hall, whereon I said,
> "To bed, Sir Bernard, get to bed.
> Two shall undress you, four with care
> Shut fast the doors, and eight up there
> Shall watch, and bid the rest beware."
> While these deceiving words I said,
> The thievish wight in terror fled.

Alteria, seeing that the hour was late and that no one was likely to solve her riddle, gave this explanation: "A gentleman had gone into the country with all his household, and had left in his palace an old woman, who prudently made a practice of going about the house at nightfall to see if she might espy any thieves, and one evening it chanced that she saw a robber on a balcony, who watched her through a hole. The good old woman refrained from crying out, and wisely made believe that her master was in the house, and a throng of servants as well. So she said: 'Go to bed, Messer Bernardo, and let two servants undress you, and four shut the doors, while eight go upstairs and guard the house.' And while the old woman was giving these orders, the thief, fearing to be discovered, stole away." When Alteria's clever riddle had been solved, Cateruzza, who was seated next to her, remembered that the third story of this first night was to be told by her, so with a smiling face she began.

THE THIRD FABLE.

Pre Scarpafico, having been once duped by three robbers, dupes them thrice in return, and lives happily the rest of his days.

THE end of Signora Alteria's story, which she has set forth with so great skill, supplies me with a theme for my own, which peradventure may please you no less than hers, though on one point it will show a variance, inasmuch as she pictured to us Pre Severino neatly entrapped by Cassandrino; while in the story I am about to tell you, Pre Scarpafico threw the net no less adroitly over divers knaves who were trying to get the better of him.

Near to Imola, a city always plagued by factious quarrels and ultimately destroyed thereby, there lived once upon a time a priest named Scarpafico, who served the village church of Postema.

He was well to do, but miserly and avaricious beyond measure, and he had for housekeeper a shrewd and clever woman named Nina, who was so alert and pushing that she would never scruple to tell any man whatever might come into her mind. And because she was faithful and prudent in administering his affairs he held her in high esteem.

Now when good Pre Scarpafico was young he was as jolly a priest as there was to be met in all the country round; but at this time age had made walking on foot irksome to him, so the good Nina was always persuading him to buy a horse, in order that his days might not be shortened through too great fatigue. At last Scarpafico, overborne by the persuasions of his servant, went one day to the market, and having seen there a mule which appeared exactly to suit his need, bought it for seven golden florins.

It happened that there were three merry fellows at the market that day, of the sort which liefer lives on the goods of others than on its own earnings—as sometimes happens even in our own time—and, as soon as they saw the bargain struck, one said to the other, 'Comrades, I have a mind that the mule yonder should belong to us.' 'But how can that be managed?' said the others. Then the first speaker replied, 'We must post ourselves along the road he will take on his journey home, about a quarter of a mile apart one from another, and as he passes each one must affirm positively that the mule he has bought is not a mule at all, but an ass, and if we are brazen enough in our declaration the mule will be ours.'

Accordingly they started from the market and stationed themselves separately on the road, as they had appointed, and when Pre Scarpafico approached the first of the thieves, the fellow, feigning to be on the road to the market, said, 'God be with you, sir!' to which Scarpafico replied, 'And welcome to you, my brother.' 'Whence come you, sir?' said the thief. 'From the market,' Scarpafico answered. 'And what good bargains have you picked up there?' asked the thief. 'This mule,' said Scarpafico. 'Which mule?' exclaimed the robber. 'Why, the mule I am riding,' returned Scarpafico. 'Are you speaking in sober truth, or do you mock me?' asked the thief; 'because it seems to me to be an ass, and not a mule.' 'Indeed,' Scarpafico answered, and without another word he went his way. Before he had ridden far he met the next robber, who greeted him, 'Good morrow, sir, and where may you come from?' 'From the market,' answered Scarpafico. 'And was there aught worth buying?' said the robber. 'Yes,' answered Scarpafico, 'I bought this mule which you see.' 'How, sir,' said the robber, 'do you mean to say you bought that for a mule, and not for an ass? What rascals must be about, seeing you have been thus cheated!' 'An ass, indeed,' replied Scarpafico; 'if anyone else should tell me this same tale, I will make him a present of the beast straightway.' Then going his way, he soon met the third thief, who said to him, 'Good morrow, sir. You come mayhap from the market?' 'I do,' replied Scarpafico. 'And what may you have bought there?' asked the robber. 'I bought this mule which I am riding,' said Scarpafico. 'Mule,' said the fellow; 'do you really mean what you say? Surely you must be joking when you call that beast a mule, while it is really an ass.' Scarpafico, when he heard this tale, said to the fellow, 'Two other men I have met told me the same story, and I did not believe them, but now it appears certain that the beast is an ass,' and having dismounted from the mule, he handed it over to the thief, who, having thanked the priest for it, went off to join his companions, leaving good Pre Scarpafico to make his way home on foot.

As soon as he came to his house he

told Nina how he had bought a nag at the market, thinking it to be a mule, but that it had proved to be an ass; and how, having been told that he had mistaken one beast for the other by several people he had met on the road home, he had given the beast to the last of them. 'Ah, you poor simpleton!' cried Nina. 'Cannot you see they have played you a trick? I thought you were cleverer than this. In truth, they would not have fooled me thus.' 'Well, it is no use to grieve over it,' said Scarpafico. 'They may have played me a trick, but see if I do not play them two in return. Be sure that these fellows, after having once fooled me, will not rest content with that, but will soon be weaving some new plot whereby they may plunder me afresh.'

Not far from Pre Scarpafico's house there lived a peasant, who had amongst his goats two which were so much alike that it was impossible to tell one from the other. These two goats the priest bought, and the next day ordered Nina to prepare a good dinner for himself and some friends he proposed to invite — some boiled veal, and roast fowls and meat, and to make savoury sauces thereto, and a tart of the sort she was accustomed to serve him with. Then he took one of the goats and tied it to a hedge in the garden, and having given it some fodder, he put a halter round the neck of the other and led it off to the market, where he was at once accosted by the three worthies of the late escapade. 'Welcome, good sir, and what may be your business here to-day? You are come, no doubt, to make another good purchase?' To which Scarpafico replied, 'I have come to buy divers provisions, for some friends are coming to dine with me; and if you will consent to join our feast it will please me greatly.' The cunning rascals willingly accepted Scarpafico's invitation, and he, when he had bought everything he required, bestowed all his purchases on the back of the goat, and said to the beast, 'Now go home and tell Nina to boil this veal, and to roast the fowls and the meat, and tell her, moreover, to make savoury sauce with these spices, and a fair tart. Do you understand? Now go in peace.' And with these words he drove off the laden goat, which, being left to go where it would, wandered away, and what befell it no one knows. Scarpafico and his companions and some other friends of his strolled about the market-place till the hour of dinner, and then they all repaired to the priest's house, where the first thing they saw on entering the garden was the goat which Scarpafico had tied to the hedge, calmly ruminating after its meal of herbage. The three adventurers at once set it down as the goat which Pre Scarpafico had despatched home with his purchases, being beyond measure amazed thereat; and when they were all come in, the priest said to Nina, 'Have you prepared everything as the goat told you?'

and she, understanding his meaning, replied, 'Yes, sir, in a few minutes the roast loin and the fowls and the boiled veal will be ready, and the sauce made with spices, and the tart likewise; all as the goat told me.'

The three robbers, when they saw set forth the roast and boiled and the tart, and heard what Nina said, were more astonished than ever, and at once began to cast about how they might get possession of the goat by theft; but when the dinner had come to an end, and they found themselves as far as ever from compassing their felonious purpose, they said to Scarpafico, 'Sir, will you do us the favour to sell us that goat of yours?' But Scarpafico replied that he had no wish to part with it, for it was worth more money than the world held; but, after a little, he consented to oblige them, and to take in exchange for it fifty golden florins. 'But,' he added, 'take warning, and blame me not afterwards if the goat does not obey you as it obeys me, for it knows you not or your ways.'

But the three adventurers heeded not this speech of Scarpafico, and, without further parley, carried off the goat, rejoicing in their bargain. When they came to their homes, they said to their wives, 'See that you prepare no food to-morrow save that which we shall send home by the goat.' On the morrow they went to the piazza, where they purchased fowls and divers other viands, and these they packed on the goat's back, and directed it to go home, and to tell to their wives all they ordered. The goat, thus laden, when it was set at liberty, ran away into the country and was never seen again.

When dinner-hour was come the three confederates straightway went home and demanded of their wives whether the goat had come back safely with the provisions, and whether they had duly cooked these according to the directions given. The women, amazed at what they heard, cried out, 'What fools and numskulls you must be to suppose that a beast like that would do your bidding! You surely have been prettily duped. With your cheating other people every day, it was quite certain you would be caught yourselves at last.'

As soon as the three robbers saw that Scarpafico had verily made fools of them, besides having eased their pockets of fifty golden florins, they were hotly incensed against him, and, having caught up their arms, they set forth to find him, swearing they would have his life. But the cunning priest, who fully expected that the robbers would seek vengeance upon him when they should discover how he had tricked them, had taken counsel with Nina thereanent. 'Nina,' he said, 'take this bladder, which you see is full, and wear it under your dress; then, when these robbers come, I will put all the blame on you, and in my rage will make believe to stab you; but I will thrust the knife in this bladder, and you must fall down as if you were dead. The rest you will leave to me.'

Scarcely had Scarpafico finished speaking when the confederates arrived, and at once made for Scarpafico as if to kill him. 'Hold, brothers,' he cried, 'what you would bring against me is none of my doing, but the work of this servant of mine, most likely on account of some affront of which I know nothing.' And, turning towards Nina, he struck his knife into the bladder, which he had previously filled with blood, and she forthwith feigned to be dead and fell down, while the blood gushed in streams about where she lay. Then the priest, looking upon his work, made great show of repentance, and bawled out lustily, 'Oh, wretched man that I am! what have I done in thus foolishly slaying this woman who was the prop of my old age? How shall I manage to live without her?' But after a little he fetched a bagpipe, made according to a fancy of

Pre Scarpafico Dupes The Robbers

Night the First

THIRD FABLE

Pre Scarpafico Dupes The Robbers

Night the First

THIRD FABLE

Pre Scarpafico Dupes The Robbers

Night the First

THIRD FABLE

his own, and blew a tune upon it, until at last Nina jumped up safe and sound, as if recalled to life.

When the robbers saw what happened they forgot their anger in their astonishment, and, after a little chaffering, they purchased the bagpipe for two hundred florins, and went highly delighted to their homes. A day or two after it chanced that one of them fell out with his wife, and, becoming enraged, stabbed her in the breast with his knife and killed her. The husband at once took the bagpipe which had been bought of Scarpafico, and blew into them as Scarpafico had done in hopes of reviving her; but he spent his wind to no purpose, for the poor woman had verily passed from this life to the next. When the second thief saw what his comrade had done, he cried out, 'What a fool you are! you have bungled the affair. Wait and see how I do it.' And with these words he seized his own wife by the hair, and cut her throat with a razor. Then, taking the bagpipe, he blew with all his might, but with no better result than the first. The third fellow, who was standing by, nothing daunted by the failure of the others, served his own wife in the same way to no better purpose; so the three were all alike wifeless. With hotter anger against Scarpafico than ever, they hurried to his house, resolved that this time they would pay no heed to his plausible tales, and seized him and thrust him into a sack, purposing to drown him in a neighbouring river. But as they bore him along something gave them an alarm, and they ran to hide themselves for a while, leaving Pre Scarpafico in his sack by the wayside.

They had not been gone many minutes before a shepherd, driving his flock to pasture, went by; and, as he drew nigh, he heard a plaintive voice saying, 'They want me to take her, but I will have none of her; for I am a priest, and have no concern with such matters.' The shepherd stopped short, somewhat frightened, because he could not discover whence came the voice, which kept repeating the same words over and over again; but, having looked now here, now there, his eye at last fell on the sack in which Scarpafico was tied up. The shepherd opened the sack and let the priest come forth, demanding why he had been thus tied up, and what he meant by the words he kept uttering. Whereupon Scarpafico declared that the seigneur of the town insisted on marrying him to one of his daughters, but that he himself had no stomach for the match, because, besides being a priest, he was too old to wive. The shepherd, who, like a simpleton, believed every word the cunning priest told him, at once cried out, 'Good father, do you think the seigneur would bestow her upon me?' 'I believe he would,' said Scarpafico, 'provided you get into this sack and let me tie you up.' The silly shepherd at once crept in, and Scarpafico, having fastened the sack, got away from the place as quickly as he could, driving the poor shepherd's flock before him.

When an hour or so had passed the three thieves returned, and, without examining the sack, they bore it to the river and threw it in, thus sending the wretched shepherd to the fate they had destined for Pre Scarpafico.

They then took their way homewards, and, as they were conversing, they perceived a flock of sheep grazing hard by, and at once began to scheme how they might easiest carry off a couple of lambs. But when they drew anigh, judge their amazement at seeing Pre Scarpafico, whom they believed to be lying at the bottom of the river, tending the flock as a shepherd. As soon as they had recovered from their amazement, they demanded of him how he had managed to get out of the river, and he straightway answered: 'Away with you! you have no more sense than so many jackasses. If you had thrown me a little farther into the stream, I should have come back with ten times as many sheep as you see here.' When the robbers heard this they cried out, 'Ah! Pre Scarpafico, will you at last do us a good turn? Will you put us into sacks and throw us into the river? Then, you see, we shall no longer have need to be footpads and rascals, and will live as honest shepherds.' 'Well,' answered Scarpafico, 'I will do so much for you; indeed, there is no favour in the world I would not grant you, on account of the love I bear you;' and, having got three good sacks of strong canvas, he tied the three thieves therein so firmly that there was no chance of their getting out, and threw them into the river. Thus they went to the place which was their due, and Scarpafico went back to Nina with good store of gold and cattle, and lived many years in happiness and prosperity.

Cateruzza's tale gave great pleasure to all the company, and won high praise, especially the part of it which dealt with Pre Scarpafico's cunning scheme whereby, in exchange for the mule he gave away, he gained much money and a fine flock of sheep. Cateruzza then set forth her enigma:

> A sturdy blacksmith and his wife,
> Who lived a simple honest life,
> Sat down to dine; and for their fare
> A loaf and a half of bread was there.
> But ere they finished came the priest,
> And with his sister joined the feast.
> The loaf in twain the blacksmith cleft,
> So three half loaves for the four were left.
> Each ate a half, each was content.
> Now say what paradox is meant.

The solution of Cateruzza's enigma was, that the blacksmith's wife was the priest's sister. When the husband and wife had sat down to their meal, the priest came in and joined them, and then, apparently, there were four of them, to wit, the blacksmith and his wife, and the priest and his sister; but in reality there were but three. As each one had a third of the bread they were all contented. After Cateruzza had explained her very ingenious enigma, the Signora gave the signal to Eritrea to give them her story, and she forthwith began.

THE FOURTH FABLE.

Tebaldo, Prince of Salerno, wishes to have his only daughter Doralice to wife, but she, through her father's persecution, flees to England, where she marries Genese the king, and has by him two children. These, having been slain by Tebaldo, are avenged by their father King Genese.

I CANNOT think there is one amongst us who has not realized by his own experience how great is the power of love, and how sharp are the arrows he is wont to shoot into our corruptible flesh. He, like a mighty king, directs and governs his empire without a sword, simply by his individual will, as you will be able to understand from the tenour of the story which I am about to tell to you.

You must know, dear ladies, that Tebaldo, Prince of Salerno, according to the story I have heard repeated many times by my elders, had to wife a modest and prudent lady of good lineage, and by her he had a daughter who in beauty and grace outshone all the other ladies of Salerno; but it would have been well for Tebaldo if she had never seen the light, for in that case the grave misadventure which befell him would never have happened. His wife, young in years but of mature wisdom, when she lay a-dying besought her husband, whom she loved very dearly, never to take for his wife any woman whose finger would not exactly fit the ring which she herself wore; and the prince, who loved his wife no less than she loved him, swore by his head that he would observe her wish.

After the good princess had breathed her last and had been honourably buried, Tebaldo indulged in the thought of wedding again, but he bore well in mind the promise he had made to his wife, and was firmly resolved to keep her saying.

However, the report that Tebaldo, Prince of Salerno, was seeking another mate soon got noised abroad, and came to the ears of many maidens who, in worth and in estate, were no whit his inferiors; but Tebaldo, whose first care was to fulfil the wishes of his wife who was dead, made it a condition that any damsel who might be offered to him in marriage should first try on her finger his wife's ring, to see whether it fitted, and not having found one who fulfilled this condition — the ring being always found too big for this and too small for that — he was forced to dismiss them all without further parley.

Now it happened one day that the daughter of Tebaldo, whose name was Doralice, sat at table with her father; and she, having espied her mother's ring lying on the board, slipped it on her finger and cried out, 'See, my father, how well my mother's ring fits me!' and the prince, when he saw what she had done, assented.

But not long after this the soul of Tebaldo was assailed by a strange and diabolical temptation to take to wife his daughter Doralice, and for many days he lived tossed about between yea and nay. At last, overcome by the strength of this devilish intent, and fired by the beauty of the maiden, he one day called her to him and said, 'Doralice, my daughter, while your mother was yet alive, but fast nearing the end of her days, she besought me never to take to wife any woman whose finger would not fit the ring she herself always wore in her lifetime, and I swore by my head that I would observe this last request of hers. Wherefore, when I felt the time was come for me to wed anew, I made trial of many maidens, but not one could I find who could wear your mother's ring, except yourself. Therefore I have decided to take you for my wife, for thus I shall satisfy my own desire without violating the promise I made to your mother.' Doralice, who was as pure as she was beautiful, when she listened to the evil designs of her wicked father, was deeply troubled in her heart; but, taking heed of his vile and abominable lust, and fearing the effects of his rage, she made no answer and went out of his presence with an untroubled face. As there was no one whom she could trust so well as her old nurse, she repaired to her at once as the surest bulwark of her safety, to take counsel as to what she should do. The nurse, when she had heard the story of the execrable lust of this wicked father, spake words of comfort to Doralice, for she knew well the constancy and steadfast nature of the girl, and that she would be ready to endure any torment rather than accede to her father's desire, and promised to aid her in keeping her virginity unsullied by such terrible disgrace.

After this the nurse thought of nothing else than how she might best find a way for Doralice out of this strait, planning now this and now that, but finding no method which gained her entire approval.

She would fain have had Doralice take to flight and put long distance betwixt her and her father, but she feared the craft of Tebaldo, and lest the girl should fall into his hands after her flight, feeling certain that in such event he would put her to death.

So while the faithful nurse was thus taking counsel with herself, she suddenly hit upon a fresh scheme, which was what I will now tell you. In the chamber of the dead lady there was a fair cassone, or clothes-chest, magnificently carved, in which Doralice kept her richest dresses and her most precious jewels, and this wardrobe the nurse alone could open. So she removed from it by stealth all the robes and the ornaments that were therein, and bestowed them elsewhere, placing in it a good store of a certain liquor which had such great virtue, that whosoever took a spoonful of it, or even less, could live for a long time without further nourishment. Then, having called Doralice, she shut her therein, and bade her remain in hiding until such time as God should send her better fortune, and her father be delivered from the bestial mood which had come upon him. The maiden, obedient to the good old woman's command, did all that was told her; and the father, still set upon his accursed design, and making no effort to restrain his unnatural lust, demanded every day what had become of his daughter; and, neither finding any trace of her, or knowing aught where she could be, his rage became so terrible that he threatened to have her killed as soon as he should find her.

Early one morning it chanced that Tebaldo went into the room where the chest was, and as soon as his eye fell upon it, he felt, from the associations connected with it, that he could not any longer endure the sight of it, so he gave orders that it should straightway be taken out and placed elsewhere and sold, so that its presence might not be an offence to him. The servants were prompt to obey their master's command, and, having taken the thing on their shoulders, they bore it away to the market-place. It chanced that there was at that time in the city a rich dealer from Genoa, who, as soon as he caught sight of the sumptuously carved cassone, admired it greatly, and settled with himself that he would not let it go from him, however much he might have to pay for it. So, having accosted the servant who was charged with the sale of it, and learnt the price demanded, he bought it forthwith, and gave orders to a porter to carry it away and place it on board his ship. The nurse, who was watching the trafficking from a distance, was well pleased with the issue thereof, though she grieved sore at losing the maiden. Wherefore she consoled herself by reflecting that when it comes to the choice of evils it is ever wiser to avoid the greater.

The merchant, having set sail from Salerno with his carven chest and other valuable wares, voyaged to the island of

Britain, known to us to-day as England, and landed at a port near which the country was spread out in a vast plain. Before he had been there long, Genese, who had lately been crowned king of the island, happened to be riding along the seashore, chasing a fine stag, which, in the end, ran down to the beach and took to the water. The king, feeling weary and worn with the long pursuit, was fain to rest awhile, and, having caught sight of the ship, he sent to ask the master of it to give him something to drink; and the latter, feigning to be ignorant he was talking to the king, greeted Genese familiarly, and gave him a hearty welcome, finally prevailing upon him to go on board his vessel. The king, when he saw the beautiful clothes-chest so finely carved, was taken with a great longing to possess it, and grew so impatient to call it his own that every hour seemed like a thousand till he should be able to claim it. He then asked the merchant the price he asked for it, and was answered that the price was a very heavy one. The king, being now more taken than ever with the beautiful handicraft, would not leave the ship till he had arranged a price with the merchant, and, having sent for money enough to pay the price demanded, he took his leave, and straightway ordered the cassone to be borne to the palace and placed in his chamber.

Genese, being yet over-young to wive, found his chief pleasure in going every day to the chase. Now that the cassone was transported into his bedroom, with the maiden Doralice hidden inside, she heard, as was only natural, all that went on in the king's chamber, and, in pondering over her past misfortunes, hoped that a happier future was in store for her. And as soon as the king had departed for the chase in the morning, and had left the room clear, Doralice would issue from the clothes-chest, and would deftly put the chamber in order, and sweep it, and make the bed. Then she would adjust the bed-curtains, and put on the coverlet cunningly embroidered with fine pearls, and two beautifully ornamented pillows thereto. After this, the fair maiden strewed the bed with roses, violets, and other sweet-smelling flowers, mingled with Cyprian spices which exhaled a subtle odour and soothed the brain to slumber. Day after day Doralice continued to compose the king's chamber in this pleasant fashion, without being seen of anyone, and thereby gave Genese much gratification; for every day when he came back from the chase it seemed to him as if he was greeted by all the perfumes of the East. One day he questioned the queen his mother, and the ladies who were about her, as to which of them had so kindly and graciously adorned his room, and decked the bed with roses and violets and sweet scents. They answered, one and all, that they had no part in all this, for every morning, when they went to put the chamber in order, they found the bed strewn with flowers and perfumes.

Genese, when he heard this, determined to clear up the mystery, and the next morning gave out that he was going to hunt at a village ten leagues distant; but, in lieu of going forth, he quietly hid himself in the room, keeping his eyes steadily fixed on the door, and waiting to see what might occur. He had not been long on the watch before Doralice, looking more beautiful than the sun, came out of the cassone and began to sweep the room, and to straighten the carpets, and to deck the bed, and diligently to set everything in order, as was her wont. The beautiful maiden had no sooner done her kindly and considerate office, than she made as if she would go back to her hiding-place; but the king, who had keenly taken note of everything, suddenly caught her by the hand, and, seeing that she was very fair, and fresh as a lily, asked her who she was; whereupon the trembling girl confessed that she was the daughter of a prince. She declared, however, that she

Princess Doralice Hiding in The King's Chest
Night the First

Princess Doralice Hiding In The King's Chest

Night the First

FOURTH FABLE

Princess Doralice Hiding In The King's Chest

Night the First

FOURTH FABLE

Princess Doralice Hiding In The King's Chest

Night the First

FOURTH FABLE

had forgotten what was his name, on account of her long imprisonment in the cassone, and she would say nothing as to the reason why she had been shut therein. The king, after he had heard her story, fell violently in love with her, and, with the full consent of his mother, made her his queen, and had by her two fair children.

In the meantime Tebaldo was still mastered by his wicked and treacherous passion, and, as he could find no trace of Doralice, search as he would, he began to believe that she must have been hidden in the coffer which he had caused to be sold, and that, having escaped his power, she might be wandering about from place to place. Therefore, with his rage still burning against her, he set himself to try whether perchance he might not discover her whereabouts. He attired himself as a merchant, and, having gathered together a great store of precious stones and jewels, marvellously wrought in gold, quitted Salerno unknown to anyone, and scoured all the nations and countries round about, finally meeting by hazard the trader who had originally purchased the clothes-chest. Of him he demanded whether he had been satisfied with his bargain, and into whose hands the chest had fallen, and the trader replied that he had sold the cassone to the King of England for double the price he had given for it. Tebaldo, rejoicing at this news, made his way to England, and when he had landed there and journeyed to the capital, he made a show of his jewels and golden ornaments, amongst which were some spindles and distaffs cunningly wrought, crying out the while, 'Spindles and distaffs for sale, ladies.' It chanced that one of the dames of the court, who was looking out of a window, heard this, and saw the merchant and his goods; whereupon she ran to the queen and told her there was below a merchant who had for sale the most beautiful golden spindles and distaffs that ever were seen. The queen commanded him to be brought into the palace, and he came up the stairs into her presence, but she did not recognize him in his merchant's guise; moreover, she was not thinking ever to behold her father again; but Tebaldo recognized his daughter at once.

The queen, when she saw how fair was the work of the spindles and distaffs, asked of the merchant what price he put upon them. 'The price is great,' he answered, 'but to you I will give one of them for nothing, provided you suffer me to gratify a caprice of mine. This is that I may be permitted to sleep one night in the same room as your children.' The good Doralice, in her pure and simple nature, never suspected the accursed design of the feigned merchant, and, yielding to the persuasion of her attendants, granted his request.

But before the merchant was led to the sleeping chamber, certain ladies of the court deemed it wise to offer him a cup of wine well drugged to make him sleep sound, and when night had come and the merchant seemed overcome with fatigue, one of the ladies conducted him into the chamber of the king's children, where there was prepared for him a sumptuous couch. Before she left him the lady said, 'Good man, are you not thirsty?' 'Indeed I am,' he replied; whereupon she handed him the drugged wine in a silver cup; but the crafty Tebaldo, while feigning to drink the wine, spilled it over his garments, and then lay down to rest.

Now there was in the children's room a side door through which it was possible to pass into the queen's apartment. At midnight, when all was still, Tebaldo stole through this, and, going up to the bed beside which the queen had left her clothes, he took away a small dagger, which he had marked the day before hanging from her girdle. Then he returned to the children's room and killed them both with the dagger, which he immediately put back into its scabbard, all bloody as it was, and having opened a window he let himself down by a cord. As soon as the shopmen of the city were astir, he went to a barber's and had his long beard taken off, for fear he might be recognized, and having put on different clothes he walked about the city without apprehension.

In the palace the nurses went, as soon as they awakened, to suckle the children; but when they came to the cradles they found them both lying dead. Whereupon they began to scream and to weep bitterly, and to rend their hair and their garments, thus laying bare their breasts. The dreadful tidings came quickly to the ears of the king and queen, and they ran barefooted and in their night-clothes to the spot, and when they saw the dead bodies of the babes they wept bitterly. Soon the report of the murder of the two children was spread throughout the city, and, almost at the same time, it was rumoured that there had just arrived a famous astrologer, who, by studying the courses of the various stars, could lay bare the hidden mysteries of the past. When this came to the ears of the king, he caused the astrologer to be summoned forthwith, and, when he was come into the royal presence, demanded whether or not he could tell the name of the murderer of the children. The astrologer replied that he could, and whispering secretly in the king's ear he said, 'Sire, let all the men and women of your court who are wont to wear a dagger at their side be summoned before you, and if amongst these you shall find one whose dagger is befouled with blood in its scabbard, that same will be the murderer of your children.'

Wherefore the king at once gave command that all his courtiers should present themselves, and, when they were assembled, he diligently searched with his own hands to see if any one of them might

have a bloody dagger at his side, but he could find none. Then he returned to the astrologer—who was no other than Tebaldo himself—and told him how his quest had been vain, and that all in the palace, save his mother and the queen, had been searched. To which the astrologer replied, 'Sire, search everywhere and respect no one, and then you will surely find the murderer.' So the king searched first his mother, and then the queen, and when he took the dagger which Doralice wore and drew it from the scabbard, he found it covered with blood. Then the king, convinced by this proof, turned to the queen and said to her, 'O, wicked and inhuman woman, enemy of your own flesh and blood, traitress to your own children! what desperate madness has led you to dye your hands in the blood of these babes? I swear that you shall suffer the full penalty fixed for such a crime.' But though the king in his rage would fain have sent her straightway to a shameful death, his desire for vengeance prompted him to dispose of her so that she might suffer longer and more cruel torment. Wherefore he commanded that she should be stripped and thus naked buried up to her chin in the earth, and that she should be well fed in order that she might linger long and the worms devour her flesh while she still lived. The queen, seasoned to misfortune in the past, and conscious of her innocence, contemplated her terrible doom with calmness and dignity.

Tebaldo, when he learned that the queen had been adjudged guilty and condemned to a cruel death, rejoiced greatly, and, as soon as he had taken leave of the king, left England, quite satisfied with his work, and returned secretly to Salerno. Arrived there he told to the old nurse the whole story of his adventures, and how Doralice had been sentenced to death by her husband. As she listened the nurse feigned to be as pleased as Tebaldo himself, but in her heart she grieved sorely, overcome by the love which she had always borne towards the princess, and the next morning she took horse early and rode on day and night until she came to England. Immediately she repaired to the palace and went before the king, who was giving public audience in the great hall, and, having thrown herself at his feet, she demanded an interview on a matter which concerned the honour of his crown. The king granted her request, and took her by the hand and bade her rise; then, when the rest of the company had gone and left them alone, the nurse thus addressed the king: 'Sire, know that Doralice, your wife, is my child. She is not, indeed, the fruit of my womb, but I nourished her at these breasts. She is innocent of the deed which is laid to her charge, and for which she is sentenced to a lingering and cruel death. And you, when you shall have learnt everything, and laid your hands upon the impious murderer, and understood the reason which moved him to slay your children, you will assuredly show her mercy and deliver her from these bitter and cruel torments. And if you find that I speak falsely in this, I offer myself to suffer the same punishment which the wretched Doralice is now enduring.'

Then the nurse set forth fully from beginning to end the whole history of Doralice's past life; and the king when he heard it doubted not the truth of it, but forthwith gave orders that the queen, who was now more dead than alive, should be taken out of the earth; which was done at once, and Doralice, after careful nursing and ministration by physicians, was restored to health.

Next King Genese stirred up through all his kingdom mighty preparations for war, and gathered together a great army, which he despatched to Salerno. After a short campaign the city was captured, and Tebaldo, bound hand and foot, taken back to England, where King Genese, wishing to know the whole sum of his guilt, had him put upon the rack, whereupon the wretched man made full confession. The next day he was conducted through the city in a cart drawn by four horses, and then tortured with red-hot pincers like Gano di Magazza, and after his body had been quartered his flesh was thrown to be eaten of ravenous dogs.

And this was the end of the impious wretch Tebaldo; and King Genese and Doralice his queen lived many years happily together, leaving at their death divers children in their place.

All the listeners were both amazed and moved to pity by this pathetic story, and when it was finished Eritrea, without waiting for the Signora's word, gave her enigma:

I tell you of a heart so vile,
So cruel, and so full of guile,
That with its helpless progeny
It deals as with an enemy.
And when it sees them plump and sleek,

It stabs them with its cruel beak.
For, lean itself, with malice fell,
It fain would make them lean as well.
So they grow thin with wasting pain,
Till nought but plumes and bones remain.

The ladies and gentlemen gave various solutions to this enigma, one guessing this and another that, but they found it hard to believe there could be an animal so vile and cruel as thus barbarously to maltreat its own progeny, but at last the fair Eritrea said with a smile, "What cause is there for your wonder? Assuredly there are parents who hate their children as virulently as the rapacious kite hates its young. This bird, being by nature thin and meagre, when it sees its progeny fat and seemly — as young birds mostly are — stabs their tender flesh with its hard beak, until they too become lean like itself."

This solution of Eritrea's pointed enigma pleased everybody, and it won the applause of all. Eritrea, having made due salutation to the Signora, resumed her seat. Then the latter made a sign to Arianna to follow in her turn, and she rising from her chair began her fable as follows.

THE FIFTH FABLE.

Dimitrio the chapman, having disguised himself as a certain Gramottiveggio, surprises his wife Polissena with a priest, and sends her back to her brothers, who put her to death, and Dimitrio afterwards marries his serving-woman.

WE often see, dear ladies, great inequality in the degree of mutual love. How often will the husband love the wife entirely, and she care little for him; and, on the other hand, the wife will love the husband to find nothing but hatred in return. In conditions like these is born the passion of sudden jealousy, the destroyer of all happiness, rendering a decent life impossible; likewise dishonourings and unseemly deaths, which often shed deep disgrace over all our sex. I will say nothing of the headlong perils, of the numberless ills, into which both men and women rush on account of this accursed jealousy. It would weary rather than divert you were I to recount them all to you one by one; but, as it is my task to bring to an end this evening of pleasant discourse, I will tell you a story of Gramottiveggio, now told for the first time, and I believe you will gather therefrom no less pleasure than edification.

The noble city of Venice, famed for the integrity of its magistrates, for the justice of its laws, and as being the resort of men from every nation of the world, is seated on the bosom of the Adriatic sea, and is named the queen of cities, the refuge of the unhappy, the asylum of the oppressed. Her walls are the sea and her roof the sky; and, though the earth produces nought, there is no scarcity of anything that life in a great city demands.

In this rich and magnificent city there lived in former days a merchant whose name was Dimitrio, a good and trustworthy man of upright life, though of low degree. He was possessed with a great desire of offspring, wherefore he took to wife a fair and graceful girl named Polissena, whom he loved as dearly as ever man loved woman, letting her clothe herself so sumptuously that there was no dame in all the city—save amongst the nobles—who could outvie her in raiment, or in rings, or in pearls of price. And besides he took care to let her have abundance of delicate victuals, which, not being suitable to one of her humble degree, gave her the look of being more pampered and dainty than she should have been.

It chanced one day that Dimitrio, who on account of his business was often constrained to travel by sea, determined to take ship with a cargo of goods for Cyprus, and, when he had got ready his apparel and stocked the house with provisions and everything that was needful, he left his dear wife Polissena with a fair and buxom serving-maid to bear her company, and set sail on his voyage.

After his departure Polissena went on living luxuriously and indulged herself with every delicacy, and before very long found she was unable to endure further the pricks of amorous appetite, so she cast her eyes upon the parish priest and became hotly enamoured of him. The priest on his part, being young, lively, and well-favoured, came at last to divine the meaning of the glances Polissena cast towards him out of the corner of her eye; and, seeing that she was gifted with a lovely face and a graceful shape, and further endowed with all the charms men desire in a woman, he soon began to return her amorous looks. Thus love grew up between them, and many days had not passed before Polissena brought the young man privily into the house to take her pleasure with him. And thus, for the course of many months, they secretly enjoyed the delights of love in close embraces and sweet kisses, letting the poor husband fare the best he might in the perils of sea and land.

Now when Dimitrio had been some time in Cyprus, and had made there a reasonable profit on his goods, he sailed back to Venice; and, having disembarked, he went to his home and to his dear Polissena, who, as soon as she saw him, burst into tears, and when Dimitrio asked her the reason of her weeping, she replied, 'I weep because of some bad news which came to me of late, and also for the great joy I feel in seeing you again; for I heard tell by many that all the ships which had sailed for Cyprus were wrecked, and I feared sorely lest some terrible misadventure should have overtaken you. But now, seeing you have by God's mercy returned safe and sound, I cannot keep back my tears for the joy I feel.' The simple Dimitrio, who had returned to Venice to make up—as he thought—to his wife for the solitary time she had passed during his long absence, deemed that the tears and sighs of Polissena sprang from her warm and constant love for him; but the poor dupe never suspected that all the while she was saying in her heart, 'Would to Heaven that he had been drowned at sea! for then I might the more safely and readily take my pleasure with my lover who loves me so well.'

Before a month had passed Dimitrio was forced to set on his travels once more, whereat Polissena was filled with joy greater than can be imagined, and forewith sent word to her lover, who showed himself to be no less on the alert; and, when the settled hour for their foregathering had come, he went secretly to her. But the comings and goings of the priest could not be kept secret enough to escape for long the eye of a certain Manusso, a friend of Dimitrio, who lived just opposite. Wherefore Manusso, who held Dimitrio in high esteem for that he was a pleasant companion and one ever ready to do a friendly service, grew mightily suspicious of his young neighbour, and kept a sharp watch over her. When he had satisfied himself that, with a given sign at a certain hour, the door would always be opened to the priest, and that after this the lovers would disport themselves with less circumspection than prudence demanded, he determined that the business, which was as yet a secret, should not be brought to light so as to stir up a scandal, but to let his project have time to ripen by awaiting the return of Dimitrio.

When Dimitrio found himself at liberty to return home, he took ship, and with a favourable breeze sailed back to Venice! and, having disembarked, went straight to his own house and knocked at the door, thus arousing the servant, who, when she had looked out of the window and recognized her master, ran quickly to let him in, weeping with joy the while. Polissena, when she heard her husband had returned, came downstairs forthwith, taking him in her arms and embracing and kissing him as if she had been the most loving wife in the world. And because he was weary and altogether worn out by the sea voyage, he went to bed without taking any food, and slept so soundly that the morning came before he had taken any amorous pleasure with his wife. When the night had passed and full daylight had come, Dimitrio awoke, and, having left the bed without bestowing so much as a single kiss upon his wife, took a little box, out of which he drew a few ornamental trinkets of no small value, which, on returning to bed, he gave to his wife, who set little store by them, seeing that her thoughts were running upon another matter. Shortly after this it happened that Dimitrio had occasion to go into Apulia to purchase oil and other merchandise, and, having announced this to his wife, he began to make ready for his journey. She, cunning and full of mischief, and feigning to be heartbroken at his departure, kissed him lovingly and besought him to tarry yet a few days longer with her; but in her heart of hearts she reckoned one day of his presence like a thousand, since it prevented her from taking her pleasure in the arms of her lover.

Now Manusso, who had often espied the priest courting Polissena and doing divers other things which it is not seemly to mention, felt that he would be working his friend a wrong if he should not now let him know all that he had seen. Therefore he determined, come what might, to tell him all. So, having invited him one day to dinner, he said to him as they sat at table, 'Dimitrio, my friend, you know, if I am not mistaken, that I have always held, and shall ever hold you in great affection, so long as there is breath in my body; nor could you name any task, however difficult, which I would not undertake for the love I bear you; and, if you would not take it ill, I could tell you of certain matters which might annoy you rather than please you, but I fear to speak lest thereby I should disturb your peace of mind. Nevertheless, if you will take it —as I hope you will—circumspectly and prudently, you will not let your anger get the mastery over you, and thus blind your eyes to the truth.' 'Know you not,' answered Dimitrio, 'that you may say to me anything you please? If you have, by any mischance, killed a man, tell me, and do not doubt my fidelity.' Manusso answered, 'I have killed nobody, but I have seen another man slay your honour and your good name.' 'Speak your meaning clearly,' said Dimitrio, 'and do not beat about the bush with ambiguous words.' 'Do you wish me to tell it you briefly?' asked Manusso; 'then listen and hear patiently what I have to say. Polissena your wife, whom you hold so dear, all the time you are away sleeps every night with a priest and takes her pleasure with him.' 'How can this be possible,' said Dimitrio, 'seeing that she loves me so tenderly, never failing when I leave her to shed floods of tears on my bosom and to fill the air with her sighs? If I were to behold this thing with my own eyes I would not believe it.' 'If you are wise, as I believe you to be,' said Manusso, 'if there is any reason in you, you will not shut your eyes, as is the way with so many simpletons and fools. I will let you see with your eyes and touch with your hands all that I have told you; then you may be convinced.' 'Then,' said Dimitrio, 'I shall be content to do whatever you may direct me in order to let you show me all you have promised.' Then Manusso replied, 'But you must take care to keep your secret and put a good face on the matter, otherwise you will wreck the whole plot.[1] When next you have to go abroad, make believe to set sail, but in lieu of quitting Venice come to my lodgings as secretly as you can, and I will clear up the mystery for you.'

[1] Orig., *altrimenti si guasterebbe la coda al fasiano.*

When the day came for Dimitrio to start on his journey he embraced his wife tenderly, while he bade her take good care of the house, and having taken leave of her feigned to go on board his ship, but turned and withdrew secretly to the lodging of Manusso. By chance it happened that, before two o'clock had struck, a terrible storm came on, with rain so heavy that it seemed as if the heavens themselves were broken up, and the rain ceased not all through the night. The priest, who had already been advertised of the departure of Dimitrio, and cared neither for wind nor rain, was waiting for the hour of assignation. When he gave the sign the door was opened to him, and, as soon as he was inside, Polissena greeted him with sweet and passionate kisses; while the husband, who was concealed in a passage over the way, saw all that went on, and, being no longer able to contradict his friend's assertion, was altogether overwhelmed, and burst into tears on account of the righteous grief which possessed him. Then said his friend to him, 'Now what do you think? Have you not seen something you would never have believed? But say not a word and keep yourself cool, for if you listen to what I have to say, and do exactly what I shall direct you, you shall see something more. Take off the clothes you are now wearing, and put on some beggar's rags, and smear your face and your hands with dirt; then go over to your own house as a beggar, and in a counterfeited voice ask for a night's lodging. Most likely the servant, seeing how bad a night it is, will take pity on you and take you in; and if you do this, you will probably see something else you would rather not see.'

Dimitrio, having listened to his friend's counsel, took off his clothes and put on instead the rags of a poor man who had come to the house and asked for lodging in God's name, and, although it still rained smartly, he went over to the door of his own house, at which he knocked thrice, weeping and groaning bitterly the while. The serving-maid having opened the window, cried out who was there, and Dimitrio, in a broken and feigned voice, replied that it was a poor old man, almost drowned by the rain, who begged a night's lodging. Whereupon the kindly girl, who was just as tender-hearted towards the poor and wretched as was her mistress towards the priest, ran to Polissena and begged her to grant the petition of this poor man who was soaked with rain, and to give him shelter till he should be warm and dry. 'He can draw us some water,' she went on, 'and make up the fire, so that the fowls may be the sooner roasted. Then I can prepare the soup, and get ready the spoons, and do other chores about the kitchen.' To this the mistress agreed, and the girl, having opened the door, let him in and bade him sit by the fire and turn the spit. It happened that the priest and Polissena, who had in the meantime been in the chamber, came down into the kitchen holding one another by the hand, and at once began to make mock of the poor wight with his dirty face. Going up to him Polissena asked what was his name. 'I am called Gramottiveggio, signora,' he replied; and Polissena when she heard this began to laugh heartily, showing all her teeth so plainly that a leech might have drawn any one of them. Then she threw her arms round the priest, crying out, 'Come, dear heart, and let me kiss you.' And poor Dimitrio had to look on while they thus kissed and embraced each other. I leave you to fancy what he felt at seeing his wife kissed and fondled by a priest in his very presence.

When the time had come for supper, the servant, when the lovers had sat down, returned to the kitchen and said to the poor man: 'Well now, father, I must just tell you that my mistress has for a husband as good a man as you would find in all Venice, one who lets her want for nothing, and God only knows where the poor man is in this dreadful weather, while she, an ungrateful hussy, caring nothing for his person and less for his honour, has let herself be blinded by this lecherous passion — always fondling this lover, and shutting the door to everybody but him alone. But, I pray you, let us go softly to the door of the chamber; then you will see what they are doing, and how they bear themselves at table.' And when they came to the door they espied the two lovers within, making good play with the viands, and carrying on all sort of amorous dalliance the while.

When the hour of bedtime came, the two lovers retired to rest, and, after a little playful pastime, began to sport in good earnest,[1] and made so much ado that the poor Dimitrio, who was abed in a chamber adjoining, did not close his eyes all night, and understood completely what was going on. As soon as morn-

[1] Orig., *cominciorono macinare à raccolta.*

ing came he repaired to the lodgings of Manusso, who, as soon as he saw him, said, laughing, 'Well, friend, how is the business going on? Is all you have seen to your taste?' 'No, indeed,' answered Dimitrio; 'I would never have believed it had I not seen it with my own eyes; but, patience! since my ill luck will have it so.' Then Manusso, who was a crafty fellow, said, 'My friend, I would have you do what I shall tell you. Wash yourself well and put on your own clothes, and go straightway to your house, and make believe that by great good luck you had not embarked before the storm broke. Take good care that the priest steal not away; for, as soon as your enter, he will assuredly hide himself somewhere, and will lie there till he can make his retreat safely. Meantime, summon all your wife's relations to a banquet at your house, and then, when you have dragged the priest from his hiding-place in their presence, you can do anything else which may seem good to you.'

Dimitrio was highly pleased at his friend's advice, and as soon as he had stripped himself of his ragged clothes went over to his house and knocked at the door. The servant, when she saw it was her master, ran forthwith to Polissena, who was yet in bed with the priest, and said to her, 'Signora, my master is come back.' Her mistress, when she heard these words, was beside herself with fright, and, getting up with what despatch she could, she hid the priest, who was in his shirt, in the coffer where she kept all her choicest raiment, and then ran in her fur-lined cloak, all shoeless as she was, to open the door to Dimitrio. 'My dear husband,' she cried, 'you are indeed welcome. I have not closed my eyes for love of you, wondering always how fortune might be using you, but God be praised for that you have come back safe and sound.' Dimitrio, as soon as he entered the chamber, said, 'Polissena, my love, I scarcely slept a wink last night on account of the bad weather, so that now I would fain rest a little; and in the meanwhile let the servant go to your brothers' house and bid them dine with us to-day.' To this Polissena replied, 'Would it not be better to wait till another day, seeing that it rains so heavily, and the girl is busy calendering our body linen and sheets and other napery?' 'To-morrow the weather will mend, and I shall have to set forth,' said Dimitrio. Polissena then said, 'But you might go yourself; or, if you are too weary, go ask your friend Manusso to do you this service.' 'That is a good suggestion,' said Dimitrio, and, having sent for his friend, he carried the affair out exactly as it had been settled.

The brothers of Polissena came, and they dined jovially together. When the table was cleared, Dimitrio cried: 'Good brothers-in-law of mine, I have never properly let you see my house, nor the fine apparel which I have given to Polissena, my wife and your sister, so that you might judge therefrom how I treat her. Now go, Polissena, my good wife, get up and show your brothers over the house.' Dimitrio then rose and showed them his storehouses full of wheat and timber and oil and other merchandise, then casks of malvoisie and Greek wine and other delicacies. Next he said to his wife: 'Bring out the rings and the pearls which I have bought for you. Just look at these fine emeralds in this little casket; the diamonds, the rubies, and other rings of price. Does it seem to you, my brothers, that your sister is well treated by me?' 'We knew all this well, brother,' they replied, 'and if we had not been satisfied with your worth, we would not have given you our sister to wife.'

But Dimitrio had not yet finished, for he next directed his wife to open all her coffers, and to bring out her fair raiment; but Polissena, her heart sinking with dread, replied, 'What need can there be to open the coffers and show my clothes? Do not my brothers know well enough that you always let me be attired full honourably — more sumptuously indeed than our station calls for?' But Dimitrio cried out, 'Open this coffer, and that, at once,' and when they were opened he went on showing all her wardrobe to her brothers.

Now when they came to the last coffer the key of this was nowhere to be found, for the good reason that the priest was hidden therein. Dimitrio, when he saw the key was not forthcoming, took up a hammer and beat the lock so lustily that it gave way, and then he opened the coffer.

The priest, shaking with fear, could in no way hide himself, or escape being recognized by all the bystanders. The brothers of Polissena, when they saw how the matter stood, were so strongly moved by anger that they were within a little of slaying her and her lover as well on the spot with the daggers they wore, but the husband was averse to this course, deeming it shameful to kill a man in his shirt, however stout a fellow he might be. He spake to the brothers thus: 'What think ye now of this trull of a wife of mine?' Then, turning to Polissena, he said: 'Have I deserved such a return as this from you? Wretched woman! who has any right to keep me back from cutting your throat?' The poor wretch, who could in no wise excuse herself, was silent, because her husband told her to her face all he had seen of her doings the night before so clearly that she could not find a word to say in her defence. Then, turning to the priest, who stood with his head bent down, he said: 'Take your clothes and go quickly from this place, and bad luck go with you. Let me never see your face again, for I have no wish to soil my hands in your accursed blood for the sake of a guilty woman. Now begone; why do you tarry?' The priest, without opening his mouth, stole away, fancying as he went that Dimitrio and his brothers-in-law were close behind him with their knives. Then, Dimitrio, turning to his brothers-in-law, said: 'Take your sister where you will, for I will not have her before my eyes any longer.' And the brothers, inflamed with rage, took her out of the house and slew her forthwith. When news of this was brought to Dimitrio, he cast his eyes on the serving-maid, who was indeed a very comely lass, and he bore in mind, moreover, the kind turn she had done him. So he made her his wife. He gave her, likewise, all the jewels and raiment of his first wife, and lived many years with her in joy and peace.

As soon as Arianna had brought her story to an end, the company with one voice cried out that the worth and the constancy of the unlucky Dimitrio was most noteworthy, even when he saw before his very eyes the priest who had wrought him this dishonour, and quite as noteworthy was the terror of the culprit, who, clad only in his shirt, and seeing the husband and brothers of his mistress close upon him, trembled like a leaf shaken by the wind. And then the Signora, perceiving that discussion on the matter promised to be overmuch, called for silence, and directed Arianna to give her enigma, whereupon she, with her gracious manner and pleasant smile, set it forth in these words:

Three jolly friends sat down to eat,
A merrier crew you could not meet.
They tried and emptied every dish,
For better fare they could not wish.
The varlet next before them placed
A dish with three fat pigeons graced.
Each ate his pigeon, bones and all,
But pigeons twain were left withal.

This enigma seemed to the company to be one very difficult to solve, and finally it was judged to be impossible, for no one saw how, after each had eaten his pigeon, two out of the three could remain on the board, but they did not look for the snake which was hidden in the grass. When, therefore, Arianna saw that the secret of her enigma had not been grasped, and that the solution was impossible, she turned her fair and delicate face towards the Signora and said: "It seems, dear lady, that my enigma is not to be solved, and yet it is not so difficult but that it may be easily disentangled. The answer is this: Out of the three jolly friends one bore the name of Each. As they sat together at the same table they ate as if they had been famished wolves, and when, at the end of the feast, the varlet brought them three roast pigeons, two out of the three revellers were so full that they could eat no more, but the one whose name was Each finished his neatly, so there were two pigeons left when they rose from the table."

The solution of this obscure riddle

was greeted with great laughter and applause, for not one of the company could have solved it. Thus, the last story of this present night having been told, the Signora directed everyone to go home to rest. And by the flare of torches, which shed over all the place a white light, the ladies and gentlemen were escorted to the landing-place.

The End of the First Night.

Night the Second.

Night the Second.

PHŒBUS had already plunged his golden wheels into the salt waves of the Indian ocean, his rays no longer gave light to the world, his horned sister now ruled the universe with her mild beams, and the sparkling stars had spread their fires thickly over the sky, when the courtly and honourable company met once more at the accustomed spot. And when they had seated themselves according to their rank, the Signora Lucretia gave the word that they should observe, this night, the same order in their entertainment as hitherto. And, seeing that five of the damsels had not told their stories, the Signora bade the Trevisan to write the names of these on paper, then to place the billets in a golden vase, and to draw them out one after another, as they had done last night. The Trevisan hastened to obey her command, and the first paper which was taken out of the vase bore the name of Isabella, the second that of Fiordiana, the third that of Lionora, the fourth that of Lodovica, and the fifth that of Vicenza. Then the flutes struck up a tune, and they all began to sing and dance in a circle, Antonio Molino and Lionora leading the revel; and they all laughed so loud and heartily, that meseems the sound of their merriment is still to be heard. And when the measure had come to an end they all sat down, and the damsels sang a fair carol in praise of the Signora.

SONG.

What once we sang we sing to-day,
And ever will we tune our lay,
To praise thee, lady, as the queen
Of beauty, and of all our bene;
The loftiest theme the poet sings,
The sweetest chord that shakes the strings,
The fairest shape the painter gives,
The peer of all in thee survives.

He who never owns the spell
Which moves us now thy praise to tell,
Wins no kindly word from me.
He the bliss shall never see
That flows on earth from faithful love,
And waits on spirits blest above.

At the close of this pleasant song Isabella, who had been chosen to begin the entertainment of the second night, began to tell the story which follows.

THE FIRST FABLE.

Galeotto, King of Anglia, has a son who is born in the shape of a pig. This son marries three wives, and in the end, having thrown off his semblance, becomes a handsome youth.

FAIR ladies, if man were to spend a thousand years in rendering thanks to his Creator for having made him in the form of a human and not of a brute beast, he could not speak gratitude enough. This reflection calls to mind the story of one who was born as a pig, but afterwards became a comely youth. Nevertheless, to his dying day he was known to the people over whom he ruled as King Pig.

You must know, dear ladies, that Galeotto, King of Anglia, was a man highly blest in worldly riches, and in his wife Ersilia, the daughter of Matthias, King of Hungary, a princess who, in virtue and beauty, outshone all the other ladies of the time. And Galeotto was a wise king, ruling his land so that no man could hear complaint against him. Though they had been several years married they had no child, wherefore they both of them were much aggrieved. While Ersilia was walking one day in her garden she felt suddenly weary, and remarking hard by a spot covered with fresh green turf, she went up to it and sat down thereon, and, overcome with weariness and soothed by the sweet singing of the birds in the green foliage, she fell asleep.

And it chanced that while she slept there passed by three fairies who held mankind somewhat in scorn, and these, when they beheld the sleeping queen, halted, and gazing upon her beauty, took counsel together how they might protect her and throw a spell upon her. When they were agreed the first cried out, 'I will that no man shall be able to harm her, and that, the next time she lie with her husband, she may be with child and bear a son who shall not have his equal in all the world for beauty.' Then said the second, 'I will that no one shall ever have power to offend her, and that the prince who shall be born of her shall be gifted with every virtue under the sun.' And the third said, 'And I will that she shall be the wisest among women, but that the son whom she shall conceive shall be born in the skin of a pig, with a pig's ways and manners, and in this state he shall be constrained to abide till he shall have three times taken a woman to wife.'

As soon as the three fairies had flown away Ersilia awoke, and straightway arose and went back to the palace, taking with her the flowers she had plucked. Not many days had passed before she knew herself to be with child, and when the time of her delivery was come, she gave birth to a son with members like those of a pig and not of a human being. When tidings of this prodigy came to the ears of the king and queen they lamented sore thereanent, and the king, bearing in mind how good and wise his queen was, often felt moved to put this offspring of hers to death and cast it into the sea, in order that she might be spared the shame of having given birth to him. But when he debated in his mind and considered that this son, let him be what he might, was of his own begetting, he put aside the cruel purpose which he had been harbouring, and, seized with pity and grief, he made up his mind that the son should be brought up and nurtured like a rational being and not as a brute beast. The child, therefore, being nursed with the greatest care, would often be brought to the queen and put his little snout and his little paws in his mother's lap, and she, moved by natural affection, would caress him by stroking his bristly back with her hand, and embracing and kissing him as if he had been of human form. Then he would wag his tail and give other signs to show that he was conscious of his mother's affection.

The pigling, when he grew older, began to talk like a human being, and to wander abroad in the city, but whenever he came near to any mud or dirt he would always wallow therein, after the manner of pigs, and return all covered with filth. Then, when he approached the king and queen, he would rub his sides against their fair garments, defiling them with all manner of dirt, but because he was indeed their own son they bore it all.

One day he came home covered with mud and filth, as was his wont, and lay down on his mother's rich robe, and said in a grunting tone, 'Mother, I wish to get married.' When the queen heard this, she replied, 'Do not talk so foolishly. What maid would ever take you for a husband, and think you that any noble or knight would give his daughter to one so dirty and ill-savoured as you?' But he kept on grunting that he must have a wife of one sort or another. The queen, not knowing how to manage him in this matter, asked the king what they should do in their trouble: 'Our son wishes to marry, but where shall we find anyone who will take him as a husband?' Every day the pig would come back to his mother with the same demand: 'I must have a wife, and I will never leave you in peace until you procure for me a certain maiden I have seen to-day, who pleases me greatly.'

It happened that this maiden was a daughter of a poor woman who had three daughters, each one of them being very lovely. When the queen heard this, she had brought before her the poor woman and her eldest daughter, and said, 'Good mother, you are poor and burdened with children. If you will agree to what I shall say to you, you will be rich. I have this son who is, as you see, in form a pig, and I would fain marry him to your eldest daughter. Do not consider him, but think of the king and of me, and remember that your daughter will inherit this whole kingdom when the king and I shall be dead.'

When the young girl listened to the words of the queen she was greatly disturbed in her mind and blushed red for shame, and then said that on no account would she listen to the queen's proposition; but the poor mother besought her so pressingly that at last she yielded. When the pig came home one day, all covered with dirt as usual, his mother said to him, 'My son, we have found for you the wife you desire.' And then she caused to be brought in the bride, who by this time had been robed in sumptuous regal attire, and presented her to the pig prince. When he saw how lovely and desirable she was he was filled with joy, and, all foul and dirty as he was, jumped round about her, endeavouring by his pawing and nuzzling to show some sign of his affection. But she, when she found he was soiling her beautiful dress, thrust him aside; whereupon the pig said to her, 'Why do you push me thus? Have I not had these garments made for you myself?' Then she answered disdainfully, 'No, neither you nor any other of the whole kingdom of hogs has done this thing.' And when the time for going to bed was come the young girl said to herself, 'What am I to do with this foul beast? This very night, while he lies in his first sleep, I will kill him.' The pig prince, who was not far off, heard these words, but said nothing, and when the two retired to their chamber he got into the bed, stinking and dirty as he was, and defiled the sumptuous bed with his filthy paws and snout. He lay down by his spouse, who was not long in falling to sleep, and then he struck her with his sharp hoofs and drove them into her breast so that he killed her.

The next morning the queen went to visit her daughter-in-law, and to her great grief found that the pig had killed her; and when he came back from wandering about the city he said, in reply to the queen's bitter reproaches, that he had only wrought with his wife as she was minded to deal with him, and then withdrew in an ill humour. Not many days had passed before the pig prince again began to beseech the queen to allow him to marry one of the other sisters, and because the queen at first would not listen to his petition he persisted in his purpose, and threatened to ruin everything in the place if he could not have her to wife. The queen, when she heard this, went to the king and told him everything, and he made answer that perhaps it would be wiser to kill their ill-fated offspring before he might work some fatal mischief in the city. But the queen felt all the tenderness of a mother towards him, and loved him very dearly in spite of his brutal person, and could not endure the thought of being parted from him; so she summoned once more to the palace the poor woman, together with her second daughter, and held a long discourse with her, begging her the while to give her daughter in marriage. At last the girl assented to take the pig prince for a husband; but her fate was no happier than her sister's, for the bridegroom killed her, as he had killed his other bride, and then fled headlong from the palace.

When he came back, dirty as usual and smelling so foully that no one could approach him, the king and queen censured him gravely for the outrage he had wrought; but again he cried out boldly that if he had not killed her she would have killed him. As it had happened before, the pig in a very short time began to importune his mother again to let him have to wife the youngest sister, who was much more beautiful than either of the others; and when this request of his was refused steadily, he became more insistent than ever, and in the end began to threaten the queen's life in violent and bloodthirsty words, unless he should have given to him the young girl for his wife. The queen, when she heard this shameful and unnatural speech, was well-nigh broken-hearted and like to go out of her mind; but, putting all other considerations aside, she called for the poor woman and her third daughter, who was named Meldina, and thus addressed her: 'Meldina, my child, I should be greatly pleased if you would take the pig prince for a husband; pay no regard to him, but to his father and to me; then, if you will be prudent and bear patiently with him, you may be the happiest woman in the world.' To this speech Meldina answered, with a grateful smile upon her face, that she was quite content to do as the queen bade her, and thanked her humbly for deigning to choose her as a daughter-in-law; for, seeing that she herself had nothing in the world, it was indeed great good fortune that she, a poor girl, should become the daughter-in-law of a potent sovereign. The queen, when she heard this modest and amiable reply, could not keep back her tears for the happiness she felt; but she feared all the time that the same fate might be in store for Meldina as her sisters.

When the new bride had been clothed in rich attire and decked with jewels, and was awaiting the bridegroom, the pig prince came in, filthier and more muddy than ever; but she spread out her rich gown and besought him to lie down by her side. Whereupon the queen bade her to thrust him away, but to this she would not consent, and spoke thus to the queen: 'There are three wise sayings, gracious lady, which I remember to have heard. The first is that it is folly to waste time in searching for that which cannot be found. The second is that we should believe nothing we may hear, except those things which bear the marks of sense and reason. The third is that, when once you have got possession of some rare and precious treasure, prize it well and keep a firm hold upon it.'

When the maiden had finished speaking, the pig prince, who had been wide awake and had heard all that she had said, got up, kissed her on the face and neck and bosom and shoulders with his tongue, and she was not backward in returning his caresses; so that he was fired with a warm love for her. As soon as the time for retiring for the night had come, the bride went to bed and awaited her unseemly spouse, and, as soon as he came, she raised the coverlet and bade him lie near to her and put his head upon the pillow, covering him carefully with the bed-clothes and drawing the curtains so that he might feel no cold. When morning had come the pig got up and ranged abroad to pasture, as was his wont, and very soon after the queen went to the bride's chamber, expecting to find that she had met with the same fate as her sisters; but when she saw her lying in the bed, all defiled with mud as it was, and looking pleased and contented, she thanked God for this favour, that her son had at last found a spouse according to his liking.

One day, soon after this, when the pig prince was conversing pleasantly with his wife, he said to her: 'Meldina, my beloved wife, if I could be fully sure that you could keep a secret, I would now tell you one of mine; something I have kept hidden for many years. I know you to be very prudent and wise, and that you love me truly; so I wish to make you the sharer of my secret.' 'You may safely tell it to me, if you will,' said Meldina, 'for I promise never to reveal it to anyone without your consent.' Whereupon, being now sure of his wife's discretion and fidelity, he straightway shook off from his body the foul and dirty skin of the pig, and stood revealed

came to the bride's chamber, expecting to find that she had met with the same [illegible] but when she saw [illegible] the bed, all defiled with [illegible], and looking pleased and [illegible], she thanked God for this [illegible], that her son had at last found a spouse according to his liking.

One day, soon after this, when the pig prince was conversing pleasantly with his wife, he said to her: "Meldina, my beloved [illegible], if I could be fully sure that [illegible]

Transformation Of The Pig Prince

Night the Second

FIRST FABLE

[illegible]

[illegible] shook off from his body the foul and dirty skin of the pig, and stood revealed

Transformation Of The Pig Prince

Night the Second

FIRST FABLE

Transformation Of The Pig Prince

Night the Second

FIRST FABLE

Transformation Of The Pig Prince

Night the Second

FIRST FABLE

as a handsome and well-shaped young man, and all that night rested closely folded in the arms of his beloved wife. But he charged her solemnly to keep silence about this wonder she had seen, for the time had not yet come for his complete delivery from this misery. So when he left the bed he donned the dirty pig's hide once more. I leave you to imagine for yourselves how great was the joy of Meldina when she discovered that, instead of a pig, she had gained a handsome and gallant young prince for a husband. Not long after this she proved to be with child, and when the time of her delivery came she gave birth to a fair and shapely boy. The joy of the king and queen was unbounded, especially when they found that the new-born child had the form of a human being and not that of a beast.

But the burden of the strange and weighty secret which her husband had confided to her pressed heavily upon Meldina, and one day she went to her mother-in-law and said: 'Gracious queen, when first I married your son I believed I was married to a beast, but now I find that you have given me the comeliest, the worthiest, and the most gallant young man ever born into the world to be my husband. For know that when he comes into my chamber to lie by my side, he casts off his dirty hide and leaves it on the ground, and is changed into a graceful handsome youth. No one could believe this marvel save they saw it with their own eyes.' When the queen heard these words she deemed that her daughter-in-law must be jesting with her, but Meldina still persisted that what she said was true. And when the queen demanded to know how she might witness with her own eyes the truth of this thing, Meldina replied: 'Come to my chamber to-night, when we shall be in our first sleep; the door will be open, and you will find that what I tell you is the truth.'

That same night, when the looked-for

time had come, and all were gone to rest, the queen let some torches be kindled and went, accompanied by the king, to the chamber of her son, and when she had entered she saw the pig's skin lying on the floor in the corner of the room, and having gone to the bedside, found therein a handsome young man in whose arms Meldina was lying. And when they saw this, the delight of the king and queen was very great, and the king gave order that before anyone should leave the chamber the pig's hide should be torn to shreds. So great was their joy over the recovery of their son that they wellnigh died thereof.

And King Galeotto, when he saw that he had so fine a son, and a grandchild likewise, laid aside his diadem and his royal robes, and advanced to his place his son, whom he let be crowned with the greatest pomp, and who was ever afterwards known as King Pig. Thus, to the great contentment of all the people, the young king began his reign, and he lived long and happily with Meldina his beloved wife.

When Isabella's story was finished, the whole company broke into laughter at the notion of the pig prince, all dirty and muddy as he was, kissing his beloved spouse and lying by her side. "But let us give over laughter," cried Signora Lucretia, "in order that Isabella's enigma may be given in due course." And forthwith Isabella, with a smile, propounded her riddle:

I prithee, sir, to give to me,
What never did belong to thee,
Or ever will, what though thy span
Of life exceed the wont of man.
Dream not this treasure to attain;
Thy longing will be all in vain;
But if you deem me such a prize,
And pine for me with loving eyes,
Give me this boon, my wish fulfil,
For you can grant it if you will.

When Isabella had set forth her cunningly devised enigma, the listeners were all in a state of bewilderment, for no one could understand how a man could give what he did not possess or ever could possess. But Isabella, when she saw that they were troubled overmuch, said: with much good taste and judgment: "There is no reason for wonder, my good friends, for a man certainly can give to a woman that which he has not or ever will have; that is to say, a man has no husband nor ever will have one, but it is an easy matter for him to give one to a lady." The whole company received this solution with much applause, and when silence had once more been imposed on the assembly, Fiordiana, who sat next to Isabella, arose from her seat and, smiling merrily, said, "Signora, and you gentle folks all, does it not seem meet to you that Signor Molino, our good friend, should enliven this honourable company with one of his merry conceits; and I say this, not because I want to escape the task of telling my own story (for I have ready more than one), but because I feel that a tale, told with all his accustomed pleasant grace and style, would, just now, give the company the greater delight. He, as you well know, is ingenious and full of wit, and gifted with all those good parts which pertain to a man of breeding. And as for ourselves, dear ladies, it is better that we should ply our needles than be always telling stories."

All agreed with these prudent and well-timed words of Fiordiana, and warmly applauded them, and the Signora, casting her eyes towards Molino, said: "Come, Signor Antonio, it is now your turn to enliven us with an example of your graceful wit." And she signed to him to begin. Molino, who had not reckoned on being named as a story-teller for this evening, first gave his thanks to Fiordiana for the flattering words she had spoken of him, and then in obedience to the Signora's direction began his fable.

THE SECOND FABLE.

Filenio Sisterno, a student of Bologna, having been tricked by certain ladies, takes his revenge upon them at a feast to which he has bidden them.

I SHOULD never have believed or imagined that the Signora would have laid upon me the task of telling a story, seeing that in the due order of things we should call upon Signora Fiordiana to give us one. But since it is the pleasure of the company, I will take upon myself to tell you something which may peradventure fit in with your humour. But if by chance my narrative (which God forbid) should prove tiresome to you, or should overstep the bounds of civility, I must crave your indulgence therefor, and that the blame may be laid on Signora Fiordiana, to whom it is in fact due.

In Bologna, the chief city of Lombardy, the parent of learning, and a place furnished with everything needful for its high and flourishing estate, there lived a young scholar of graceful and amiable parts named Filenio Sisterno, born in the island of Crete. It chanced one day that a magnificent feast was given, to which were invited the most beautiful and distinguished ladies of Bologna, and many gentlemen, and certain of the scholars, amongst whom was Filenio. After the manner of gallants, he went dallying now with this and now with that fair dame, and finding no difficulty in suiting his taste, resolved to lead out one of them for a dance. His choice fell upon the Signora Emerentiana, the wife of a certain Messer Lamberto Bentivogli, and she, who was very gracious, and no less sprightly than beautiful, did not say him nay. During the dance, which Filenio took care should be very gentle and slow, he wrung her hand softly, and thus addressed her in a whisper: 'Ah! Signora, how great is your beauty; surely it transcends any that has yet met my eye; surely the lady does not live who could ensnare my heart as you have ensnared it. If only I might hope you would give me back the like, I should be the happiest man in the world; but if you should prove cruel, you will soon see me lying dead at your feet, and know yourself as the cause of my bane. Seeing that I love you so entirely — and indeed I could do no other thing — you ought to take me for your servant, disposing both of my person and of the little I can call mine as if they were your own. Higher favour from heaven I could not obtain than to find myself subject to such a mistress, who has taken me in the snare of love as if I had been a bird.' Emerentiana, while she listened earnestly to these sweet and gracious speeches, like a modest gentlewoman made as though she had no ears, and held her peace. When the measure had come to an end, Emerentiana sat down, and straightway Filenio led out another lady as his partner, but the dance had scarcely begun before he began to address her in like fashion: 'Of a truth, most gracious Signora, there is no need for me to waste words in setting forth how deep and ardent is the love I have for you, and ever shall have, so long as this soul of mine inhabits and rules my unworthy frame. And I would hold myself blest indeed if I could possess you as the lady of my heart and my peculiar mistress. Therefore, loving you as I do, and being wholly yours, as you may easily understand, I beg you will deign to take me for your most humble servant, seeing that my life and everything I have to live for depends on you and on no other.' The young lady, whose name was Panthemia, although she understood all this, made no reply, but modestly went on with the dance, and, when it had come to an end, she sat down with the other ladies, smiling a little the while.

But short time had passed before the gallant scholar took a third partner by the hand; this time the most seemly, the most gracious, and the fairest lady in Bologna, and began to tread a measure with her, making all those who pressed round to admire her, give way; and before the dance was ended he thus addressed her: 'Most estimable lady, perhaps I shall seem to you out of measure presumptuous to reveal the secret love which I have borne, and still bear towards you, but for this offence blame not me, but your own beauty, which raises you high above all others, and makes me your slave. I speak not now of your delightful manners, nor of your surpassing virtues, which are great enough and many enough to bring all the world to your feet. If then your loveliness, the work of nature, and owing nought to art, fascinates everyone, there is no wonder that it should constrain me to love you and to guard your image in my inmost heart. I beseech you then, sweet lady, the one comfort of my life, to spare some tenderness for one who dies for you a thousand times a day. If you grant me this grace I shall know I owe my life to you; so to your kindness I now recommend myself.'

The fair lady, who was called Sinforosia, when she heard the sweet and loving words which came from Filenio's ardent bosom, could not forbear sighing, but taking heed of her honour as a married woman she answered him nought, and when the dance was come to an end returned to her seat.

It happened that all these three ladies found themselves sitting in a ring close to one another, and disposed for sprightly talk, when Emerentiana, the spouse of Messer Lamberto, moved by jocund humour and not by spite, said to her two companions, 'Dear friends, I have to tell you of a diverting adventure which has this evening befallen me.' 'And what is it?' they inquired. Said Emerentiana, 'This evening, in the course of the dancing, I have gotten for myself a cavalier, the handsomest, the trimmest, the most gracious you could find anywhere, who protests himself to be so hotly inflamed with my beauty that he can find no rest day or night.' And word by word she related all that the scholar had said to her. As soon as Panthemia and Sinforosia heard her story, they told her that the same had happened to them, and before they left the feast they had satisfied themselves that it was the same gallant who had made love to all three of them. Wherefore they clearly comprehended that the words of this gallant sprang not from loyal feeling, but from deceit and feigning of love, and they gave to them no more credence than one is wont to give to the babblings of a sick man or to the romancer's fables, and they did not go from thence before they had agreed, each one of them, to put a trick upon him such as he would not readily forget; for ladies, too, may play jokes.

Filenio meantime was bent on amorous design, and went on making love, now to one lady now to another. Judging from their carriage that they looked not unkindly upon him, he set himself the task, if it were possible, of moving each one of them to grant him the supremest favour of love, but the issue of the affair was not according to his desire, for all his schemes went astray.

Emerentiana, who could no longer bear with the mock love-making of the silly scholar, called to a pretty buxom handmaid of hers, and charged her to find some excuse for speaking with Filenio, in order to disclose to him the love which her mistress had conceived for him, and to let him know that he might whenever he would spend a night with her in her own house. When Filenio heard this he was much elated, and said to the maid, 'Hasten home forthwith and commend me to your mistress, and tell her in my behalf that she may expect me this evening at her house, provided that her husband be not at home.' When this word had been brought to Emerentiana, she straightway caused to be collected a great store of prickly thorns, and having strewn these under the bed where she lay at night, she awaited the coming of her gallant. When it had become dusk the scholar took his sword and stole towards the house of his fancied mistress, and the door, when he had given the password, was immediately opened. Then, when the two had held some little converse and supped daintily, they withdrew into the bedchamber for the night.

Scarcely had Filenio taken off his clothes to go to bed when Messer Lamberto was heard without, and hereupon the lady, feigning to be at her wits' end where she should hide her lover, bade him get under the bed. Filenio, seeing how great the danger was, both to the lady and to himself, made haste to betake himself thither, without putting on any more clothes than the shirt he wore, and was in consequence so grievously pricked by the thorns prepared for him that there was no part of his body, from the crown of his head to the sole of his foot, which was not running with blood. And the more he essayed in this dark hole to defend himself from the pricks, the more grievously was he wounded, and he dared not make a sound lest Messer Lamberto should hear him and slay him. I leave you to figure in what plight the poor wretch found himself that night, seeing that he dared not call out, though he was like to lose a good part of his breech through the torment he was suffering. When the morning was come, and the husband had left the house, the wretched scholar clothed himself as best he could, and made his way back to his lodging, bleeding and in great fear lest he should die. But being well treated by his physician, he got well and recovered his former health.

Many days had not passed before Filenio essayed another bout of love-making, casting amorous eyes on the other two ladies, Panthemia and Sinforosia, and went so far as to find one evening an occasion to address Panthemia, to whom he rehearsed his continued woes and torments, and besought her that she would have pity upon him. Panthemia, who was full of tricks and mischief, while feigning to compassionate him, made excuse that it was not in her power to do his will; but at last, as if vanquished by his tender prayers and ardent sighs, she brought him into her house. And when he was undressed, and ready to go to bed with her, she bade him go into a cabinet adjacent, where she kept her orange water and perfumes, to the intent that he might well perfume his person, and then go to bed. The scholar, never suspecting the cunning of this mischief-working dame, entered the cabinet, and having set his foot upon a board unnailed from the joist which held it up, he and the board as well fell down into a warehouse below, in which certain merchants kept their store of cotton and wool, and although he fell so far he suffered no ill. The scholar, finding himself in this dark place, began to search for some ladder or door to serve his exit, but coming upon none he cursed the hour and the place where he had first set eyes on Panthemia. The morning dawned at last, and then the unhappy wight began to realize by degrees the full treachery of Panthemia. He espied on one side of the storehouse certain outlets in the wall, through which streamed in a dim light, and, finding the masonry to be old and moss-grown, he set to work with all his strength to pull out the stones in the spot which had fallen most to decay, and soon made a gap big enough to let him out. And, finding himself in an alley, clad only in his shirt, and stockingless, he stole back to his lodging without being seen of any.

And next it happened that Sinforosia, having heard of the tricks which the two others had played the scholar, resolved to treat him with a third, no less noteworthy; so, the next time she saw him, she began to ogle him with the tail of her eye, by way of telling him that a passion for him was burning her up. Filenio, forgetting straightway his former mishaps, began to walk up and down past her house, and play the lover. Sinforosia, when she saw from this that he was deeply smitten with love for her, sent him a letter by an old woman to let him know that he had so completely captured her fancy by his fine person and gracious manners that she could find rest neither night nor day, and to beg him that, whenever it might please him, he would come and hold converse with her, and give her a pleasure greater than any other. Filenio took the letter, and having mastered the contents, was at once filled with more glee and happiness than he had ever known before, clean forgetting all the tricks and injuries he had suffered hitherto. He took pen and ink, and wrote a reply, that, though she might be enamoured of him, he, on his part, was just as much in love with her, or even more, and that at any time she might appoint he would hold himself at her service and commands. When she had read this reply, Sinforosia made it her business to find full soon an opportunity for the scholar to be brought to her house, and then, after many feigned sighs, she said: 'O my Filenio, of a truth I know of no other gallant who could have brought me into such plight, but you alone; since your comeliness, your grace, and your discourse have kindled such fire in my heart that I burn like dry wood.' The scholar, while he listened, took it for certain that she was melting with love for him, and, poor simpleton as he was, kept on some time bandying sweet and loving words with her, till it seemed to him that the time had come to go to bed and to lie down beside her. Then Sinforosia said: 'Before we go to bed it seems meet that we should regale ourselves somewhat. And having taken him by the hand, she led him into an adjoining cabinet, where there was a table spread with sumptuous cakes and wines of the finest, in which the mischievous dame had caused to be mingled a certain drug, potent to send her gallant to sleep for a certain time. Filenio took a cup and filled it with wine, and suspecting no fraud he emptied it straightway. Enlivened by the banquet, and having washed himself in orange water and dainty perfumes, he got into bed, and then immediately the drug began to work, and he slept so sound that even the uproar of great artillery would scarce have awakened him. Then, when Sinforosia perceived that he was in a heavy slumber and that the drug was doing its work well, she called one of her maids, a strong wench whom she had made privy to the jest, and the two of them took Filenio by the legs and arms, and, having opened the door softly, they placed him in the street, about a stone's cast from the house, and there left him.

It was about an hour before dawn when, the drug having spent its force, the poor wretch came to himself, and, believing that he had been in bed with the lady, found himself instead stockingless, and clad only in his shirt, and half dead with cold through lying on the bare ground. Almost helpless in his arms and legs, he found it a hard matter to get on his feet, and, when he had done so much, it was with difficulty that he kept from falling again; but he managed, as best he could, to regain his lodging and to care for his health. Had it not been for his lusty youth, he would surely have been maimed for life; but he regained his former health, and when he went abroad again he showed no signs of remembering his injuries and vexations which had been put upon him; but, on the other hand, he bore himself toward the three ladies as if he loved them as well as ever, and feigned, now to be enamoured of one, and now of another. The ladies, never suspecting malice on his part, put a good face on the matter, and treated him graciously as if they were dealing with a real lover. Filenio was many times tempted to give his hand free play, and to mark their faces for them, but he prudently took thought of the condition of the ladies, and of the shame that would be cast on him should he offer violence to them, and he restrained his wrath. Day and night he considered how he might best wreak his vengeance on them, and when he could hit on no plan he was in great perplexity. But in the course of time he devised a scheme by which he might readily work his purpose, and fortune aided him to prosecute it as he designed. He hired for himself in the city a very fine house, containing a magnificent hall and many dainty chambers, and in this he purposed to give a great and sumptuous feast, and to invite thereto a company of gentlefolk, Emerentiana, and

Panthemia, and Sinforosia amongst the rest. They accepted the scholar's invitation without demur, suspecting nothing sinster in the same, and when they were come to the feast the wily scholar led them with many courteous speeches into a room and begged them to take some refreshment. As soon as the three ladies—foolish and imprudent indeed—had entered the room, Filenio locked the door, and, advancing towards them, said: 'Now, my pretty ladies, the time is come for me to take my revenge upon you, and to give you some repayment for all the ills you put upon me, just because I loved you so well.' When they heard these words, they seemed more dead than alive, and began to repent heartily that they had ever abused him, and at the same time to curse their own folly in having trusted the word of one they ought to have treated as a foe. Then the scholar with fierce and threatening looks commanded them that they should, if they set any store on their lives, strip themselves naked, and the ladies, when they heard this speech, exchanged glances one with the other and began to weep, begging him the while, not only for the sake of love, but also for the sake of his natural gentleness, that their honour might be left to them. Filenio, exulting in his deed, was exceedingly polite to them, but at the same time informed them that he could not suffer them to remain clothed in his presence. Hereupon the ladies cast themselves down at Filenio's feet, and with piteous weeping humbly besought him not to be the cause of so great shame to them. But he, whose heart was now grown as hard as a stone, cried out that what he would do to them was in no sense blameworthy: it was nothing but just revenge; so the ladies were forced to take off their clothes and to stand as naked as when they were born, in which condition they appeared fully as fair as when apparelled. When this had come to pass even Filenio began to feel some pity for them; but, remembering his recent wrongs, and the mortal perils he had undergone, he chased away his pitying humour and once more hardened his heart. He then craftily conveyed all the clothes and linen they had lately worn into a neighbouring cabinet, and bade them with threatenings all to get into one bed. The ladies, altogether astounded and shaking with terror, cried out, 'Wretched fools that we are! What will our husbands and our friends say when it shall be told to them that we have been found here slain in this shameful case?' The scholar, seeing them lying one by the other like married folk, took a large sheet of linen, very white, but not fine enough to suffer their bodies to be seen and recognized, and covered them therewith from head to foot; then he left the chamber, locking the door behind him, to go and find the three husbands, who were dancing in the hall. Their dance being finished, Filenio led them with him into the chamber where the ladies were lying in the bed, and said to them: 'Gentlemen, I have brought you hither for your diversion, and to show you the prettiest sight you have ever seen;' and, having led them up to the bed with a torch in his hand, he began softly to lift up the covering at their feet, and to turn it back so as to disclose the fair limbs beneath it as far as the knees, thus giving the three husbands something wondrous fair to look upon. Next he uncovered them as far as their stomachs, which he then disclosed entirely by lifting the sheet in the same way. I leave you to imagine how great was the diversion the three gentlemen got from this jest of Filenio's, also in what distressful plight these poor wretched ladies found themselves when they heard their husbands join in mocking them. They lay quite still, not daring even to cough, lest they should be discovered, while their husbands kept urging the scholar to uncover their faces; but he, wiser in other men's wrongs than in his own, would not oblige them so far. Not content with this, he brought forth their garments, which he showed to their husbands, who, when they looked thereon, were astonished and somewhat perturbed at heart, and, after examining them closely, said one to another: 'Is not this the gown which I once had made for my wife?' 'Is not this the coif which I bought for her?' 'Is not this the pendant that she hangs round her neck? Are not these the rings she wears on her fingers?'

At last Filenio brought the three gentlemen out of the chamber, and bade them, so as not to break up the company, to remain to supper. The scholar, learning that the supper was ready and everything set in order by the majordomo, gave the word for everyone to take his place. And while the guests were setting their teeth to work, Filenio returned to the chamber where the three ladies were, and as he uncovered them said: 'Good evening, fair ladies; did

Filenio Sisterno's Revenge

Night the Second

SECOND FABLE

Filenio Sisterno's Revenge

Night the Second

SECOND FABLE

Filenio Sisterno's Revenge

Night the Second

SECOND FABLE

you hear what your husbands were saying? They are now without, waiting impatiently to see you. Get up; surely you have slept enough; give over yawning and rubbing your eyes. Take your clothes and don them without delay, and go into the hall where the other guests await you.' With such words as these he mocked them; while they, disconsolate and despairing, feared lest this adventure might come to some fatal issue, and wept bitterly. At last, full of anguish and terror, and looking for nothing less than death at his hands, they arose and turning to the scholar said to him: 'Filenio, you have taken more than vengeance upon us. Now nothing remains but for you to draw your sword and make an end of our lives, for we desire death beyond any other thing. And if you will not grant us this boon, at least suffer us to return unobserved to our homes, so that our honour may be saved.'

Filenio, seeing that he had carried the

affair far enough, gave them back their garments, and directed them to clothe themselves quickly, and when this was done he sent them out of the house by a secret door, and they went back to their homes. At once they laid aside their fine clothes, which they had lately worn, and put them away in their presses, and with great prudence sat down to work instead of going to bed. When the feast had come to an end, the three husbands thanked the scholar for the fine entertainment he had given them, and in particular for the sight of the beauties laid out for their benefit in the chamber, beauties surpassing the sun himself, and, having taken leave of him, they returned to their homes, where they found their wives sewing beside the hearth. Now the sight of the clothes, and the rings, and the jewels, which the scholar had exhibited to them, had made them somewhat suspicious: so each one now demanded of his wife where she had spent that evening, and where her best garments were. To this questioning each lady replied boldly that she had not left the house that evening, and, taking the keys of the coffers wherein was disposed her apparel, she showed this to her husband, with the rings and other jewels which he had given her. When the husbands saw these they were silent, and knew not what to say, but after a little they told their wives word by word what they had seen that evening. The ladies made as if they knew nothing of it, and, after jesting a little over the matter, they undressed and went to bed. And in after times Filenio often met the three ladies in the streets, and would always inquire of them: 'Which of you was in the greatest fear? and did I suffer most from your jests, or you from mine?' But they always held their eyes down on the ground, and said nothing. And in this fashion the scholar avenged himself as well as he could of the tricks he had suffered, without violence or outrage.

When they had listened to the story of Molino, the Signora and all the other ladies declared that the revenge, worked upon the three gentlewomen by the scholar for the tricks they had played him, was no less revolting than cowardly; but when they came to consider the severe punishment which the poor fellow had suffered in couching upon the thorns, and the danger of breaking his bones he had incurred in falling down into the warehouse, and the biting cold he had been exposed to when laid out in the open street upon the bare earth clad only in his shirt, they admitted that his vengeance was no heavier than was due. The Signora, though she had excused Fiordiana from telling her story in due order, now demanded of her that she should at least give her enigma, which ought to have some reference to the story of the scholar; and she, in obedience to this word, said: 'Signora, it happens that the enigma which I have to submit to the company has nothing in keeping with deeds of grave and terrible vengeance such as the ingenious Signor Antonio has set forth in his fable, but at the same time it will be one which may be of interest to every studious youth.' And without further delay she propounded her enigma :

From two dead blocks a living man
Gave life to one whose spirit ran
To vivify another wight,
Who thus from darkness rose to light.
Two living ones together bide,
The creature by the maker's side,
And by the creature's radiance led,
The master communes with the dead.

This subtle riddle of the Signora Fiordiana was interpreted in various wise, but not one of the company hit upon its exact meaning. And seeing that Fiordiana kept on shaking her head at the essays made by the company, Bembo remarked with a quiet smile, " Signora Fiordiana, it seems to me to be foolishness to waste our time in this fashion. Tell us what you will, and we shall be contented." " Since this noble company decrees," replied Fiordiana, "that I should be my own interpreter, I will gladly do this; not because I deem myself in any way competent for this task, but because I wish to oblige all you here, to whom I am bound by so many kindnesses. My enigma shows simply a student who rises from bed early in the morning, and he, a living thing, by the working of two dead things, the flint and the steel, gives life to the dead tinder, and this in its turn enlivens the dead candle. Thus the first living one, the student, by the help of these other two living ones who lately were dead, sits down to converse with the dead, that is, with the books writ by learned men of times long past." The explication of this most ingenious riddle by Fiordiana pleased the company greatly, and the Signora directed Lionora to begin her story at once.

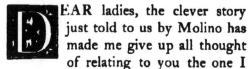

THE THIRD FABLE.

Carlo da Rimini vainly pursues Theodosia with his love, she having resolved to live a virgin. In striving to embrace her he meets with divers misadventures, and is well beaten by his own servants to boot.

DEAR ladies, the clever story just told to us by Molino has made me give up all thought of relating to you the one I had in my mind, and to offer in its place another which, if I am not mistaken, will be equally pleasing to you ladies as Molino's was to the gentlemen. Mine will certainly be shorter than his, and, I think I may say, more decent in the subject it treats.

I must tell you then that Carlo da Rimini—as I think many of you know —was a man whose trade was fighting, a despiser of God, a blasphemer of the saints, brutal and a cutthroat, and at the same time given over to all kinds of effeminate luxury. So great indeed was his malignity and the corruption of his nature, that his equal could not be found. Now in the days when he was a handsome, seemly young man, it chanced that he became hotly enamoured of a certain maiden, the daughter of a poor widow, who, though she was very poor and only contrived to find a living for herself and her child with much difficulty, would rather have died with hunger than have consented to live on the wages of her daughter's sin.

The maiden, whose name was Theodosia, was very fair and graceful in her person, and no less honest and discreet in her conduct; moreover, she was of a prudent, sober temper, and had already determined to devote herself to the religious life and to prayer, holding all worldly things to be of small account. Carlo, therefore, burning with lascivious passion, was in the habit of molesting her with his attentions every day, and on any day when he might not chance to see her he was like to die of vexation.

With flatteries and gifts and solicitations he made frequent trial to win the maiden's consent to his wishes, but all his importunities were in vain; for, like a wise and good girl, she would have none of his presents, and every day she prayed to God to turn away from his heart these dishonest wishes. At last there came a time when he could no longer hold within bounds his ardent lust and bestial desire, and, feeling gravely affronted at these continual rebuffs by one whom he loved more dearly than his own life, he made up his mind to ravish her and satisfy his lecherous appetite, let the consequence be what it might. But he feared to stir up a commotion through any public scandal, lest the people, who held him in great hatred, should rise and slay him.

But at last, being overcome by his unbridled desire, with his mind distempered with rage as if he had been a mad dog, he made a plan with two of his underlings — desperate ruffians both of them — to carry her off and then to ravish her. Therefore one day, when the evening dusk had fallen, he armed himself and went with the two desperadoes to the young girl's dwelling-place, the door of which he found open; but before entering he charged his men to keep on the alert, and to take care, as they valued their own lives, that no other person should enter the house or come out therefrom until he himself should rejoin them. The two ruffians, who were full willing to obey their leader's behests, gave answer that whatever he might command should be carried out.

But Theodosia (by some means unknown to me) had got tidings of Carlo's intent, and had shut herself up in a small kitchen, and Carlo, when he had mounted the staircase of the poor little house, found there the old mother, who, suspecting nothing of any such surprise, had taken to her spinning. He demanded forthwith where was her daughter, for whom he had such great love and desire, and the poor old woman, as soon as she perceived that the young lecher was fully armed and manifestly more inclined to evil than to good, was greatly confounded in her mind, and her face became as white as the face of a corpse, and she was on the point of screaming aloud; but, perceiving that her outcries would be of no use, she determined to hold her peace, and put her honour in the keeping of God, whom she altogether trusted. So, plucking up her courage, she turned to Carlo and said: 'Carlo, I know not what humour or what insolent spirit may have brought you here to defile the soul of this girl, who desires to live honestly. If by chance you should be come with righteous intent, then may God grant you fulfilment of every just and honourable wish; but if it should be otherwise, which God forbid, you are guilty of a great wickedness in trying to attain by outrage that which can never be yours. Therefore, cast away and have done with this unbridled lust, and no longer strive to ravish from my daughter that which you can never give back to her, to wit, the chastity of her body. And the more you lust after her, the more she will hate you, seeing that her mind is firm set to dedicate herself to virginity.'

Carlo, when he heard these moving words spoken by the poor old mother, instead of being awakened to pity or turned away from his evil intent, raged like a madman, and began to search for Theodosia in every corner of the house, without finding any trace of her, until he came to the little kitchen, where, seeing that the door was fast close, he thought (and thought rightly) that she must be concealed. Then, spying through a crack in the door, he perceived Theodosia, who was at her prayers, and with honeyed words he began to beseech her that she would open to him the door, addressing her in these terms: 'Theodosia, life of my life, be sure that I am not come here to sully your honour, which is more dear to me than my own self and my own good name, but to take you as my wife, provided that my offer be acceptable to you and to your good mother. And, beyond this, I swear I will have the life of anyone who may in any way affront your honour.'

Theodosia, who listened attentively to Carlo's speech, answered him straightway in these terms: 'Carlo, I beseech you to give over this obstinate prosecution of your desire. I can never marry you, seeing that I have offered my virginal service to Him who sees and governs us all. And if cruel fortune should suffer you to defile violently this body of mine, at least you will have no power to blacken the purity of my soul, which from the hour of my birth I have dedicated to my Creator. God has given you freedom of will so that you may know the evil from the good, and may do that which seems best to you. Follow, therefore, after the good, and you will be of good report, and turn aside from evil.' Carlo, when he found that his flattery availed him nothing, and that the maiden refused to have aught to say to him, could no longer keep under the fire which was burning in his heart, and, more maddened than ever, trusted no longer to words, but resorted to violence, bursting open by force the door, which, being none of the strongest, soon gave way as he willed.

When Carlo entered the little kitchen and cast his eyes upon the maiden, so full of grace and fair beyond belief, his passion grew hotter than ever, and, thinking only of satisfying to the full his inordinate lust, he threw himself upon her from behind, just as if he had been an eager famishing greyhound, and she a timid hare. And the ill-fated Theodosia, with her golden hair loose over her shoulders, and grasped tightly round the neck by Carlo, grew pale, and felt so deadly a languor coming over her that she could scarcely move. Then she commended her soul to heaven and demanded help of God above, and scarcely had she finished her mental prayer, when, in miraculous wise, her body seemed to melt away out of Carlo's grip; and at the same time God dazzled so completely his eyesight and understanding that he no longer knew rightly what were the things around him, and while he deemed he was holding the maid in his embrace and covering her with kisses and endearments, he was, in sooth, embracing nothing better than the pots and pans, spits and cauldrons, and other kitchen gear lying about the place. Though his lust was in some measure satisfied, he soon felt his wounded heart stirring again, and again he flew to embrace a huge kettle, fancying all the while that he held in his arms the fair form of Theodosia. In thus handling the kettles and cauldrons his hands and face were so besmirched with soot that he looked less like Carlo da Rimini than the devil. In the end, feeling that his desire was for the nonce satisfied, and conscious that it was time to retreat, he made his way out by the staircase all blackened as he was, but the two ruffians, who were keeping guard near the door lest anyone should enter or leave the house, when they saw him thus transformed, with his face all disfigured, and looking more like a beast than a human being, imagined that he must be some ghost or evil spirit, and were fain to take to their heels and save themselves from this monster. But having taken heart to stand up to him, and to look closely into his face, which seemed to them mightily disfigured and ugly, they began to drub him with cudgels and with their fists, which were as hard as iron, so that they mangled cruelly his face and his shoulders with hearty good-will, and left not a hair on his head. Not content with this, they threw him down on the ground, stripping off the clothes from his back, and dealing him as many kicks and cuffs as he could endure, and the blows fell so thick and fast that Carlo had no time allowed him to open his mouth and ask the reason of his cruel chastisement. Nevertheless, he made shift at last to break away from their hold, when he ran as for his life, always suspecting, however, that the ruffians were close behind him.

Thus Carlo, having been soundly beaten [1] by his servants, his eyes being so discoloured and swollen from their lusty pummelling that he could scarcely see, ran towards the piazza, clamouring and complaining loudly of the ill-handling he had got from his own men. The town-guard, when he heard these shouts and lamentations, went towards him, and, marking his disfigured state and his face all bedaubed with dirt, took him for a madman. And since no one recognized him, the whole crowd began to mock at him, and to cry: 'Give it to him,

[1] Orig., *essendo da suoi servi senza pettine oltra modo carminato.*

give it to him, for he is a lunatic.' Then some hustled him, others spat in his face, and others took dust and cast it in his eyes; and they kept on maltreating him thus for a good space of time, until the uproar came to the ears of the prætor, who, having risen from his bed and gone to the window which overlooked the piazza, demanded what had happened to cause so great a tumult. One of the guards thereupon answered that there was a madman who was turning the piazza topsy-turvy, and the prætor gave order that he should be securely bound and brought before him, which command was forthwith carried out.

Now Carlo, who up to this time had been the terror of all, finding himself thus bound and ill-treated and insulted, without a notion as to the cause of it, was utterly confounded in his mind, and broke out into so violent a rage that he well nigh burst the bonds that held him. But as soon as he was brought before the prætor, the latter recognized him straightway as Carlo da Rimini, and at once set down the filthy condition of his prisoner as the work of Theodosia, for he was privy to the fact that Carlo was inflamed with passion for the girl. Therefore he at once began to use soft speech and to soothe Carlo, promising to make smart sharply those who had brought upon him such a shameful mischance. Carlo, who suspected not that his face was like that of a blackamoor, could not at first gather the purport of these words, but in the end, when it had been known to him how filthy his condition was, how that he resembled a brute beast rather than a man, he, like the prætor, attributed his discomfiture to Theodosia, and, letting his rage have free course, he swore an oath that unless the prætor would punish her he would take revenge by his own hand. When the morning was come, the prætor sent for Theodosia, deeming that she had wrought this deed by magic arts. But she gave good heed to the plight in which she stood, and completely realized the great danger thereof; so she betook herself to a convent of nuns of holy life, where she abode secretly, serving God for the rest of her days with a cheerful heart.

It happened after this that Carlo was sent to lay siege to a strong place, and, when in the assault he pressed on to a more desperate essay than he had power to accomplish, he found himself caught like a rat in a trap; for, as he mounted the walls of the citadel to plant thereon the banner of the Pope, he was smitten by a great stone, which crushed him and dashed him to pieces in such manner that no time was allowed to him to make his peace with heaven. Thus the wicked Carlo made a wretched end of his days, according to his deserts, without having plucked that fruit of love he desired so ardently.

Before Lionora had come to the end of her concisely-told fable, all her good companions began to laugh over the stupidity of Carlo in kissing and embracing the pots and kettles, thinking all the while that he was enjoying his beloved Theodosia; nor did. they make less merry in the case of the cuffs and blows he got from the hands of his own men in the rough handling they gave him. And after a good spell of laughter Lionora, without waiting for further word from the Signora, set forth her enigma:

I am fine and pure and bright,
At my best am snowy white.
Maid and matron scourge and flout me,
Yet they cannot do without me,
For I serve both young and old,
Shield their bodies from the cold.
A parent mighty mothered me,
Mother of all mothers she.
And, my time of service past,
I'm torn and beaten at the last.

This cleverly-worded enigma won the praise of all the company, but since it seemed to be beyond the power of anyone to solve it, Lionora was requested to divulge its meaning; whereupon she said with a smile: "It is scarcely becoming that one of parts so slender as mine should presume to teach you, ladies and gentlemen, who are so much better versed in knowledge. But since this is your will, and since your will to me is law, I will tell you forthwith what I mean by my enigma. It means nothing else than linen cloth, fine and white, which is by ladies pierced by scissors and needles, and beaten. And it serves as a covering to us all, and comes from the mother of us all, the earth; moreover, when it grows old we no longer send it to the fuller, but let in be torn up small and made into paper."

Everyone was pleased with the interpretation of this clever enigma and commended it highly. The Signora having already remarked that Lodovica, who was chosen to tell the next story, was troubled with a bad headache, turned to the Trevisan and said, "Signor Benedetto, it is indeed the duty of us ladies to provide the stories to-night; but seeing that Lodovica is gravely troubled in her head, we beg you to take her place this evening, and grant you free field to tell whatever may please you best." To which speech the Trevisan thus replied: "It happens, Signora, that I am little skilled in these matters; nevertheless (since your will commands my entire obedience) I will use my best effort to satisfy you all, begging you at the same time to hold me excused if I fail therein." And having made due salutation, he rose from his seat and began his story in the following words:

THE FOURTH FABLE.

The devil, having heard divers husbands railing over the humours of their wives, makes trial of matrimony by espousing Silvia Balastro, and, not being able to endure his wife for long, enters into the body of the Duke of Malphi.

THE frivolity and want of judgment which nowadays is to be found amongst most women (I speak of those who, without heed, give full license to their eyes and fancy in straining to compass their unbridled lust), offers me occasion to tell to this noble concourse a story which may not be familiar. And, although you may find it somewhat short, and ill put together, it may, nevertheless, serve as a wholesome lesson to you wives to be less irksome and exacting to your husbands than you have been heretofore. And if I seem to lay on the lash too heavily, blame not me, who am but the humble servant of all you others, but make your complaint to the Signora, who, as you have heard, has given me leave to set before you whatever story might commend itself to my taste.

I will first tell you, gracious ladies, that many years ago the devil, becoming weary of the unceasing and clamorous accusations made by husbands against their wives, determined to test the truth of these by making trial of marriage himself, and, that he might the better compass this design, he took the shape of a goodly young man of courtly manners, and well furnished with lands and gold, Pancrazio Stornello by name. As soon as the bruit of his intention got abroad in the city, divers matchmakers waited upon him with plentiful choice of comely women, well dowered, for his wife, and from amongst these he settled upon Silvia Balastro, a noble maiden. Never before had the city witnessed such magnificent nuptials and rejoicings. The kinsfolk of the bride came from far and near, and for the best man the bridegroom chose one Gasparino Boncio, a townsman of repute. A few days after the marriage the devil addressed Sylvia, saying, 'My dear wife, I need scarcely tell you that I love you better than I love myself, seeing that I have already given you many tokens of my affection; therefore, for the sake of this love of mine, I am about to beg of you a favour which will be easy for you to grant, and most acceptable to me. This favour is nought else than that you should demand of me all that you want now, and all that you will ever be likely to want, of raiment, jewellery, pearls, and other things of the same sort which ladies love; for I have determined, on account of the great love I have for you, to give you all you may demand, though it may cost a kingdom. I make but one condition, which is, that you shall never trouble me about such matters again; so be careful that you get all you can possibly require for the rest of our married life, and be careful likewise never to demand aught of me more, for you will ask in vain.' Silvia begged for time to consider this proposition, and, having betaken herself to Signora Anastasia, her mother, a worldly-wise old lady, she laid bare the offer of her husband, and asked for advice thereanent. Anastasia, who knew well enough how to play a game of this sort, took pen and paper and wrote out a list of articles, such as would need two days to describe by word of mouth, and said to Silvia, 'Take this paper, and ask your husband to give you everything that is here written down. If he agrees, you may be well content with him.' Hereupon Silvia departed, and, having found her husband, she asked him to give her all that was written on the list, and he, when he had carefully read it over, said, 'Are you quite sure, dearest Sylvia, that you have put down here all you want — that there is nothing missing for which at some future time you may have to ask me? for I warn you that, if this should be so, neither your prayers nor your sighs nor your tears will avail to get it for you.'

Silvia could think of nothing else to ask for, and agreed to the conditions of her husband, who at once commanded to be made vast store of rich vestments studded with big pearls, and rings and all sorts of jewels the most sumptuous that were ever seen. And over and above these he gave her coifs and girdles embroidered with pearls, and all manner of other dainty baubles which can be better imagined than described. When Silvia was arrayed in these, and conscious of being the best dressed woman in the city, she became somewhat saucy. There was nothing else she could ask her husband for, so well had he cared for her needs.

It chanced, soon after this, that the city was all agog concerning a great feast to which were bidden all the nobles of the place, and amongst these was naturally included Silvia, who was amongst the most beautiful and distinguished ladies in the city. And the more to honour this festival, the other ladies met and devised all sorts of new fashions of dress, altering them so much that anyone accoutred in those in vogue heretofore would hardly have been recognized. There was no mother's daughter in the town — just as if it had happened to-day — who was not bent on mounting the newest fashion to do honour to the festival, and each one vied to outdo the other in pomp and magnificence.

When there came to Silvia's ears the news that the fashion of dress was to be changed, she was at once beset with fear that the store of raiment she had lately received from her husband would be found of unfashionable shape and unfit to be worn at the feast, and, in consequence, fell into a melancholy humour, neither eating nor sleeping, and making the house resound with her sighs and groans. The devil, who fathomed the trouble in his wife's heart, feigned to know nothing of it, and one day addressed her: 'What is troubling you, Silvia, that you look so unhappy? Have you no heart for the coming festival?' Silvia, seeing her opportunity, plucked up courage and said: 'What is the festival to me? How can I go there in these old-fashioned clothes of mine? I am sure you will not force me thither to be mocked at by the others.' Then said Pancrazio to her: 'Did I not give you everything you would want for the rest of your days? How comes it that you now ask me for more after agreeing to the conditions I then made?' These words only made Silvia weep the more, and, bewailing her unhappy fate, cry out that she could not go to the feast because she had no clothes fit to wear. Then said the devil, 'I gave you at first all that was necessary for the rest of your days, but I will once more gratify your wishes. You may ask of me for anything you want, and your request shall be granted; but never again. If, after this, you make a like petition, the issue will be something you will never forget.'

Silvia straightway put off her peevish humour, and wrote out another list of braveries as long as the last, which Signor Pancrazio procured for her without delay. In the course of time the ladies of the city once more set to work to make another change in the fashion of dress, and once more Silvia found herself clad in dresses of out-worn cut. No other lady could boast of jewels so costly, or of robes of such rich and sumptuous web; but this was no solace to her, and she went mourning all day long, without daring to make another appeal to her husband, who, marking her tristful face, and knowing well enough what was vexing her, said, 'Silvia, my love, why are you so sad?' Then she took courage and said, 'Is there not cause enough for me to be sad, seeing that I have no raiment in the new fashion, and that I cannot show my face amongst the other ladies of the city without their making a mock of me, and bringing reproach upon you as well as upon myself? and the respect and fidelity I have towards you do not merit such a return of shame and humiliation.' At these words the devil was terribly wroth and said: 'What cause have you for complaint? Have I not twice over given you all you have asked for? Your desires are insatiable, and beyond my power to satisfy. I will once more give you everything you may demand, but I will straightway go away and you will never see my face again.' The devil was as good as his word, and, after he had given Silvia a goodly store of new garments, all after the latest fashion, he left her without taking leave of her, and went to Malphi, where, for a diversion, he entered into the body of the duke and tormented him grievously.

Now it chanced that, soon after this, Gasparino Boncio, the gallant who had acted at Pancrazio's nuptials as best man, was forced to fly from his city on account of some offence against good manners. Wherefore he betook himself to Malphi, where he managed to live by gambling and by a lot of cunning tricks of which he was master, and rumour would have it that he was a man of parts, though he was indeed nought but a sorry knave. One day, when at the cards with some gentlemen of the place, he went a step too far, and roused their wrath so hotly that, but for fear of the law, they would certainly have made an end of him. One of these, smarting under some special wrong, vowed that he would bring Master Gasparino into such a plight as he would never forget. And forthwith he betook himself to the duke, and, having made a profound obeisance, he said: 'Your excellency, there is in this town a man named Gasparino, who makes boast that he can cast out evil spirits — whether of this world or of the nether one — which may have entered the bodies of men; therefore, methinks, you would do wisely to bid him try his skill to deliver you from your torment.' On hearing these words the duke sent forthwith for Gasparino, who, being summoned, went into the duke's presence at once.

'Signor Gasparino,' said the duke, 'they tell me you profess to be an exorcist of evil spirits. I, as no doubt you have heard, am sorely tormented by one of these, and I pledge my faith to you that, if you will work your spells upon him and drive him out, I will deal with you so that you may live for the rest of your days free from care.' Gasparino was utterly confounded by this speech, and, as soon as the duke was silent, he began to stammer and to protest loudly that he knew nought of such matters, and had never boasted of any such power; but the gentleman, who was standing by, came forward and said: 'Do you not remember, Signor Gasparino, that, on a certain day, you told me this and that?' Gasparino persisted in denying any such speech, and, while they were wrangling together, the duke broke in and said: 'Come, come, hold your peace, both of you! As for you, Master Gasparino, I give you three days to work up your charms, and, if you can deliver me from this misery, I promise you the most beautiful castle in my dominions, and you may ask of me whatever you will. But, if you fail in this, before eight days have passed I will have you strangled between two of these columns.'

Gasparino, when he listened to the duke's command, was utterly confounded and filled with grief, and, having withdrawn from the duke's presence, began to ruminate day and night as to how he might accomplish the task laid upon him. On the day fixed for the incantation he went to the palace, and, having ordered to be spread on the floor a large carpet, began to conjure the evil spirit to come out, and to cease his torment. The devil, who was quite at his ease in the duke's body, did not reply, but breathed so strong a blast of wind through the duke's throat that he was like to choke him. When Gasparino renewed his conjurations the devil cried out: 'My friend, you can enjoy your life; why can't you leave me at peace here, where I am very comfortable? Your mummery is all in vain.' And here the devil began to deride him. But Gasparino was not to be daunted by this, and for the third time he called upon the devil to come out, asking him so many questions that at last he got to know the evil spirit to be no other than his whilom friend, Pancrazio Stornello. 'And I know you, too,' the devil went on; 'you are Gasparino Boncio, my very dear friend. Don't you remember those merry nights we spent together?' 'Alas! my friend,' said Gasparino, 'why have you come here to torment this poor man?' 'That is my secret,' answered the devil; 'why do you refuse to go away and leave me here, where I am more at my ease than ever I was before?' But Gasparino went on with his questioning so long and so adroitly that he induced the devil at last to tell him the story of his wife's insatiable greed, of the violent aversion he had conceived for her thereanent, and how he had fled from her and taken up his abode in the body of the duke, and that no consideration would induce him to return to her. Having learned so much, Gasparino said: 'And now, my dear friend, I want you to do me a favour.' 'What may it be?' the devil inquired. 'Nothing more than to get you gone from the body of this poor man.' 'Friend Gasparino,' quoth the devil, 'I never set you down as a wise man, but this request of yours tells me you are a downright fool.' 'But I beg you, I implore you for the sake of the merry bouts we have enjoyed together, to do as I ask,' said Gasparino. 'The duke has heard that I have power to cast out spirits, and has imposed this task upon me. Unless I fulfil it I shall be hanged, and you will be chargeable with my death.' 'Pooh!' said the devil, 'our camaraderie lays no such duties upon me. You may go to the lowest depths of hell for all I care. Why didn't you keep your tongue between your teeth, instead of going about boasting of powers you do not possess?' And with this he roared most horribly, and threw the poor duke into a fit which nearly made an end of him.

But after a little the duke came to

himself again, and Gasparino thus addressed him: 'My lord, take courage; for I see a way of ridding you of this evil spirit. I must ask you to command all the players of music in the city to assemble at the palace to-morrow morning, and at a set moment to strike their instruments, while the bells all ring loudly, and the gunners let off their cannon as a sign of rejoicing for victory. The more noise they make the better for my purpose. The rest you may leave to me.'

The next morning Gasparino went to the palace, and duly began his incantations, and, as it had been settled, the trumpets and cymbals and tambours gave out their music, and the bells and artillery clanged and roared so loud and long that it seemed as if the uproar would never cease. At last the devil asked Gasparino, 'Isn't there a hideous medley of sound about the place? What is the meaning of it? Ah, I begin to hear it plain now!' 'Begin to hear it!' said Gasparino. 'Surely there has been clamour enough for the last half-hour to have deafened even you.' 'I dare say,' the devil replied; 'but you must know that the bodies of you mortals are gross and dull enough to shut out the sound from the hearing of one in my place; but, tell me, what is the reason of this noise?' 'I'll tell you in a very few words,' said Gasparino, 'if in the meantime you let the duke have a little ease.' 'It shall be as you wish,' said the devil. And then Gasparino brought out his story.

'You must know, my dear friend and former comrade,' he began, 'that it has come to the duke's ears how you were forced to run away from your wife on account of the woes you suffered through her greed for attire, and he has in consequence invited her to Malphi. The noise you hear is part of the rejoicing of the city over her arrival.' 'I see your hand in this, honest Signor Gasparino,' said the devil. 'Well, you have outdone me in cunning. Was there ever a loyal friend? Was I not right in belittling the claims of comradeship? However, you have won the game. The distaste and horror in which I hold my wife are so great that I will do your bidding and betake myself elsewhere; indeed, rather than set eyes on her again, I prefer to depart for the nethermost hell. Farewell, Gasparino, you will never see me or hear of me again.'

Immediately after these words the poor duke began to throttle and choke, and his eyes rolled about in ghastly wise; but these frightful tokens only gave warning that the evil spirit had at last taken flight. Nothing remained to tell of his presence save an appalling smell of sulphur. Gradually the duke came to himself, and, when he had regained his former health, he sent for Gasparino, and, to prove his gratitude, gave him a stately castle, and a great sum of money, and a crowd of retainers to do him service. Though assailed by the envy of certain of the courtiers, Gasparino lived happily for many years; but Silvia, when she saw all the treasures her husband had given her turn to smoke and ashes, lost her wits, and died miserably.

The Trevisan told his story with great wit, and the men greeted it with hearty applause and laughter; but the ladies demurred somewhat thereat, so that the Signora, hearing them murmuring amongst themselves while the men kept on their merriment, commanded silence and directed the Trevisan to give his enigma, and he, without excusing himself to the ladies for the sharp pricks against their sex dealt out in his story, thus began:

In our midst a being proud
Lives, with every sense endowed.
Keen his wit, though brainless he,
Reasoning with deep subtlety.
Headless, handless, tongueless too,
He kens our nature through and through.
Born but once and born for ever,
Death shall touch or mar him never.

The abstruse riddle of the Trevisan was no light task for the wit of the company, and it was in vain that each one essayed its unravelling. At last the Trevisan, seeing that his guesses were all wide of the mark, said: "It does not seem meet for me to perplex any longer the ingenuity of this honourable company. By your leave I will now unfold its meaning, unless you had rather wait for some cunning wit to fathom it." With one voice they prayed him to unveil its purport, and this he did in these terms: "My enigma signifies nothing else than the immortal soul of man, which, being spiritual, has neither head nor hands nor tongue, yet it makes its working known to all, and, whether it be judged in heaven or in hell, lives eternally." This learned unfolding of the Trevisan's obscure riddle pleased the company vastly.

Inasmuch as the night was now far spent, and the clamour of the cocks foretelling the dawn was heard, the Signora made sign to Vicenza, who was bespoken to tell the finishing story of the second night, to begin her task. But Vicenza, red in the face through choler at the Trevisan's story, and not from bashfulness, cried out: "Signor Benedetto, I looked for a better turn from you than this, that you would aim at something higher than the character of a mere railer against women; but since you take so bitter a tone, meseems you must have been vexed by some lady who has asked more of you than you could give. Surely you lack justice if you judge us all alike; your eyes will tell you that some of us, albeit all of the same flesh and blood, are gentler and more worshipful than others. If you rate us in such wise, wonder not if some day you find your beauty marred by some damsel's finger-nails. Then you will sing your songs in vain."

To her the Trevisan replied: "I did not tell my story to hurt the feelings of anyone, nor for spite of my own; but to give counsel and warning to those ladies who may be going to marry, to be modest and reasonable in the calls they make on their husbands." "I care nought what may have been your object," said Vicenza, "nor do these ladies either; but I will not sit silent and let it be thought I allow these charges of yours against women to have any worth. I will tell you a story which you may find to be one for your own edification," and having made obeisance she began.

THE FIFTH FABLE.

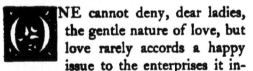

Messer Simplicio di Rossi is enamoured of Giliola, the wife of Ghirotto Scanferla, a peasant, and having been caught in her company is ill-handled by her husband therefor.

ONE cannot deny, dear ladies, the gentle nature of love, but love rarely accords a happy issue to the enterprises it inflames us to undertake. And thus it fell out in the case of the lovesick Messer Simplicio di Rossi, who, when he flattered himself that he was about to enjoy the person of the woman he desired so ardently, had to fly from her laden with as many buffets as he well could carry. All this history I will duly set forth, if, as is your gracious custom, you will lend your ears to the fable I purpose to relate to you.

In the village of Santa Eufemia, situated just below the plain of San Pietro, in the territory of the famous and illustrious city of Padua, there lived, some years ago, one Ghirotto Scanferla, a man rich and influential enough for a man in his station, but at the same time a factious, wrangling fellow, and he had for a wife a young woman named Giliola, who, albeit that she was peasant born, was very fair and graceful. With her Simplicio di Rossi, a citizen of Padua, fell violently in love. Now it happened that he had a house which stood not far removed from that of Ghirotto, and he was accustomed frequently to roam about the neighbouring fields with his wife, a very beautiful lady, whom however he held in but little esteem, although she had many good qualities which ought to have bound him to her. So great was his passion for Giliola that he got no rest day or night, but he let this passion lie closely hidden in his heart, partly because he feared lest he might in any way arouse the husband's wrath, partly on account of Giliola's good name, and partly for fear of giving offence to his own wife. Now close to Messer Simplicio's house there was a fountain from which gushed forth a stream of water, much sought by all the people round, and so clear and delicious that even a dead man might have been tempted to drink thereof; and hither every morning and evening Giliola would repair, with a copper pail, to fetch water for her household needs. Love, who of a truth spares nobody, spurred on Messer Simplicio in his passion; but he, knowing what her life was and the good name she bore, did not venture to manifest his love by any sign, and simply sustained himself and comforted his heart by gazing now and then upon her beauty. For her part she knew nothing of all this, nor was she cognizant at all of his admiration; for, as became a woman of honest life, she gave heed to nothing else but to her husband and her household affairs.

Now one day it happened that Giliola, when she went according to her custom to fetch water, met Messer Simplicio, to whom she said, in her simple, courteous way, as any woman might, 'Good morrow, Signor,' and to this he replied by uttering the word 'Ticco.' His thought was to divert her somewhat by a jest of this sort, and to make her familiar with his humour. She, however, took no heed thereof, nor said another word, but went straightway about her business. And as time went on the same thing happened over and over again, Simplicio always giving back the same word to Giliola's greeting. She had no suspicion of Simplicio's craftiness, and always went back to her home with her eyes cast down upon the ground; but after a time she determined that she would tell her husband what had befallen her. So one day, when they were conversing pleasantly together, she said to him, 'Oh! my husband, there is something I should like to tell you, something that perhaps will make you laugh.' 'And what may this thing be?' inquired Ghirotto. 'Every time I go to the well to draw water,' said Giliola, 'I meet Messer Simplicio, and when I give him the good morning he answers to me "Ticco." Over and over again I have pondered over this word, but I cannot get at the meaning thereof.' 'And what answer did you give him?' said Ghirotto, and Giliola replied that she had answered him nothing. 'Well,' said Ghirotto, 'take care that when he next says "Ticco" to you you answer him "Tacco." See that you give good heed to this thing I tell you, and be sure not to say another word to him, but come home according to your wont.' Giliola went at the usual time to the well to fetch the water, and met Messer Simplicio and gave him good day, and he, as hitherto, answered her 'Ticco.' Then Giliola, according to her husband's directions, replied 'Tacco,' whereupon Messer Simplicio, suddenly inflamed, and deeming that he had at last made his passion known to her, and that he might now have his will of her, took further courage and said, 'And when shall I come?' But Giliola, as her husband had instructed her, answered nothing, but made her way home forthwith, and being questioned by him how the affair had gone, she told him how she had carried out everything he had directed her to do; how Messer Simplicio had asked her when he might come, and how she had given him no reply.

Now Ghirotto, though he was only a peasant, was shrewd enough, and at once grasped the meaning of Messer Simplicio's watchword, which perturbed him mightily; for it struck him that this word meant more than mere trifling.[1] So he said to his wife, 'If the next time you go to the well he should ask of you, "When shall I come?" you must answer him, "This evening." The rest you can leave to me.'

The next day, when Giliola went according to her wont to draw water at the well, she found there Messer Simplicio, who was waiting for her with ardent longing, and greeted him with her accustomed 'Good morning, Signor.' To this the gallant answered 'Ticco,' and she followed suit with 'Tacco.' Then he added, 'When shall I come?' to which she replied, 'This evening.' 'Let it be so then,' he said. And when Giliola returned to her house she said to her husband, 'I have done everything as you directed.' 'What did he answer?' said Ghirotto. 'He said he would come this evening,' his wife replied.

[1] Orig., *infilzar perle al scuro.*

Now Ghirotto, who by this time had got a bellyful of something else besides vermicelli and maccaroni, spake thus to his wife: 'Giliola, let us go now and measure a dozen sacks of oats, for I will make believe that I am going to the mill, and when Messer Simplicio shall come, you must make him welcome and give him honourable reception. But before this, have ready an empty sack beside those which will be full of oats, and as soon as you hear me come into the house make him hide himself in the sack thus prepared, and leave the rest to me.' 'But,' said Giliola, 'we have not in the house enough sacks to carry out the plan you propose.' 'Then send our neighbour Cia,' said the husband, 'to Messer Simplicio to beg him to lend us two, and she can also let it be known that I have business at the mill this evening.' And all these directions were diligently carried out. Messer Simplicio, who had given good heed to Giliola's words, and had marked, moreover, that she had sent to borrow two of his sacks, believed of a truth that the husband would be going to the mill in the evening, and found himself at the highest pitch of felicity and the happiest man in the world, fancying the while that Giliola was as hotly inflamed with love for him as he was for her; but the poor wight had no inkling of the conspiracy which was being hatched for his undoing, otherwise he would assuredly have gone to work with greater caution than he used.

Messer Simplicio had in his poultry yard good store of capons, and he took two of the best of these and sent them by his body-servant to Giliola, enjoining her to let them be ready cooked by the time when he should be with her according to their agreement. And when night had come he stole secretly out and betook himself to Ghirotto's house, where Giliola gave him a most gracious reception. But when he saw the oat-sacks standing there he was somewhat surprised, for he expected that the husband would have taken them to the mill; so he said to Giliola, 'Where is Ghirotto? I thought he had gone to the mill, but I see the sacks are still here; so I hardly know what to think.' Then Giliola replied, 'Do not murmur, Messer Simplicio, or have any fear. Everything will go well. You must know that, just at vesper-time, my husband's brother-in-law came to the house and brought word that his sister was lying gravely ill of a persistent fever, and was not like to see another day. Wherefore he mounted his horse and rode away to see her before she dies.' Messer Simplicio, who was indeed as simple as his name imports, took all this for the truth and said no more.

Whilst Giliola was busy cooking the capons and getting ready the table, lo and behold! Ghirotto her husband appeared in the court-yard, and Giliola, as soon as she saw him, feigned to be grief-stricken and terrified, and cried out, 'Woe to us, wretches that we are! We are as good as dead, both of us;' and without a moment's hesitation she ordered Messer Simplicio to get into the empty sack which was lying there; and when he had got in—and he was mightily unwilling to enter it—she set the sack with Messer Simplicio inside it behind the others which were full of oats, and waited till her husband should come in. And when Ghirotto entered and saw the table duly set and the capons cooking in the pot, he said to his wife: 'What is the meaning of this sumptuous supper which you have prepared for me?' and Giliola made answer: 'I thought that you must needs come back weary and worn out at midnight, and, in order that you might fortify and refresh yourself somewhat after the fatigues you so constantly have to undergo, I wished to let you have something succulent for your meal.' 'By my faith,' said Ghirotto, 'you have done well, for I am somewhat sick and can hardly wait to take my supper before I go to bed, and moreover I want to be astir in good time to-morrow morning to go to the mill. But before we sit down to supper I want to see whether the sacks we got ready for the mill are all in order and of just weight.' And with these words he went up to the sacks and began to count them, and, finding there were thirteen, he feigned to have made a miscount of them, and began to count them over again, and still he found there were thirteen of them; so he said to his wife: 'Giliola, what is the meaning of this? How is it that I find here thirteen sacks while we only got ready twelve? Where does the odd one come from?' And Giliola answered: 'Yes, of a certainty, when we put the oats into the sacks there were only twelve, and how this one comes to be here I cannot tell.'

Inside the sack, meantime, Messer Simplicio, who knew well enough that there were thirteen sacks on account of his being there, kept silent as a mouse and went on muttering paternosters beneath his breath, at the same time cursing Giliola, and his passion for her, and his own folly in having put faith in her. If he could have cleared himself from his present trouble by flight, he would have readily taken to his heels, for he feared the shame that might arise thereanent, rather than the loss. But Ghirotto, who knew well enough what was inside the sack, took hold of it and dragged it outside the door, which he had by design left open, in order that the poor wretch inside the sack, after he should have been well drubbed, might get out of the sack and have free field to go whithersoever he listed. Then Ghirotto, having caught up a knotty stick which he had duly prepared for the purpose, began to belabour him so soundly that there was not a square inch of his carcass which was not thrashed and beaten; indeed, a little more would have made an end of Messer Simplicio. And if it had not happened that the wife, moved by pity or by fear lest her husband should have the sin of murder on his soul, wrenched the cudgel out of Ghirotto's hand, homicide might well have been the issue.

At last, when Ghirotto had given over his work and had gone away, Messer Simplicio slunk out of his sack, and, aching from head to foot, made his way home, half dreading the while that Ghirotto with his stick was close behind him; and in the meantime Ghirotto and his wife, after eating a good supper at Messer Simplicio's cost, went to bed. And after a few days had passed, Giliola, when she went to the well, saw Simplicio, who was walking up and down the terrace in his garden, and with a merry glance greeted him, saying, 'Ticco, Messer Simplicio;' but he, who still felt the pain of the bruises he had gotten on account of this word, only replied:

Neither for your good morning, nor for your tic nor your tac,
Will you catch me again, my lady, inside your sack.

When Giliola heard this she was struck silent, and went back to her house with her face red for shame, and Messer Simplicio, after the sorry usage he had received, changed his humour and gave the fullest and most loving service to his own wife, whom he had hitherto disliked, keeping his eyes and his hands off other men's goods, so that he might not again be treated to a like experience.

When Vicenza had made an end of her story, all the ladies cried out with one voice: "If the Trevisan treated badly the women he dealt with in his fable, Vicenza has in hers given the men yet worse measure in letting Messer Simplicio be thus beaten and mauled in the mishandling he got." And while they were all laughing, one at this thing and another at that, the Signora made a sign for silence in order that Vicenza might duly propound her enigma; and the latter, feeling that she had more than avenged the insult put upon her sex by the Trevisan, gave her enigma in these terms:

I blush to tell my name aright,
Rough to touch, and rude to sight.
Wide and toothless is my mouth,
Red of hue my lips uncouth;
Black all round, and from below
Ardour oft will make me glow;
Rouse my passion closely pent,
Make me foam till I am spent.
A scullion base may e'en abuse me,
And all men at their pleasure use me.

The men were hard pressed to keep from laughing when they saw the ladies cast down their eyes into their laps, smiling somewhat the while. But the Signora, to whom modest speech was more pleasing than aught that savoured of ribaldry, bent a stern and troubled glance upon Vicenza and thus addressed her: "If I had not too much respect for these gentlemen, I would tell you to your face what really is the meaning of this lewd and immodest riddle of yours; but I will forgive you this once, only take good heed that you offend not again in such fashion; for, if you should, I will let you feel and know what my power over you really is." Then Vicenza, blushing like a morning rosebud at hearing herself thus shamefully reproved, plucked up her courage and gave answer in these terms; "Signora, If I have uttered a single word which has offended your ears, or the ears of any of the modest gentlewomen I see around me, I should assuredly deserve not only your reproof, but severe chastisement to boot. But, seeing that my words were in themselves simple and blameless, they scarcely merited so bitter a censure; for the interpretation of my riddle, which has been apprehended by you in a mistaken sense, will show my words to be true and prove my innocence at the same time. The thing which my enigma describes is a stockpot, which is black all round, and when fiercely heated by the fire boils over and scatters foam on all sides. It has a wide mouth and no teeth, and takes everything that may be thrown into it, and any scullion may take out what he will when the dinner is being prepared for his master."

When they heard from Vicenza this modest solution of her riddle, all the listeners, men as well as women, gave her hearty praise, deeming the while that she had been wrongfully reproved by the Signora. And now, because the hour was late, and the rosy tints of morning already visible in the sky, the Signora, without excusing herself in any way for the scolding she had given Vicenza, dismissed the company, bidding them all under pain of her displeasure to assemble in good time the following evening.

The End of the Second Night.

Night the Third.

Night the Third.

ALREADY the sister of the sun had begun her reign in the sky over the forests and the gloomy gorges of the hills, and showed her golden circle over the half of heaven; already the car of Phœbus had sunk beneath the western wave, the moving stars had lighted their lamps, and the pretty birds, ceasing their pleasant songs and bickerings, sought repose in their nests set amongst the green boughs, when the ladies and the gallant youths as well met on the third evening in the accustomed spot to renew their story-telling. And as soon as they were all seated according to their rank, the Signora Lucretia commanded that the vase should be brought forth as before, and in it she caused to be placed the names of five damsels, who, according to the order determined by lot, should that evening tell in turn their stories. The first name which was drawn from the vase was that of Cateruzza, the second that of Arianna, the third that of Lauretta, the fourth that of Alteria, and the fifth that of Eritrea. Then the Signora gave the word for the Trevisan to take his lute, and Molino his viol, and for all the rest to tread a measure to Bembo's leading. And when the dance had come to an end, and the sweet lyre and the divine strings of the hollow lute were silent, the Signora directed Lauretta to begin her song, and she, anxious to obey the Signora in everything, took hands with her companions, and having made respectful salutation, sang in clear and mellow tone the following song:

SONG.

Lady, while thy face I scan,
Where love smiling holds his court,
Lo! from out your beauteous eyes

Light so radiant doth arise,
That it shows us Paradise.

All my sighs and all my tears,
Which I foolish shed in vain;
All the anguish of my heart,
All my hidden woe and smart,
With my faint desire have part.

Then to love's last mood I fly,
Recking nought that earth and sky
Stand beneath me and above;
So my soul is drawn by love
To the heights of passion free,
And I learn that fate's decree
Binds me, whatsoe'er betide,
Dead or living, to thy side.

After Lauretta and her companions had given sign by their silence that their song had come to an end, the Signora, bending her gaze upon the fair and open countenance of Cateruzza, said that the task of making a beginning of the story-telling of that third evening fell upon her, and Cateruzza, with a becoming blush upon her cheek and laughing lightly, began in these terms.

THE FIRST FABLE.

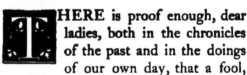

A simple fellow, named Peter, gets back his wits by the help of a tunny fish which he spared after having taken it in his net, and likewise wins for his wife a king's daughter.

THERE is proof enough, dear ladies, both in the chronicles of the past and in the doings of our own day, that a fool, whether by lucky accident or by sheer force of blundering, may sometimes score a success where a wise man might fail. Therefore it has come into my mind to tell you the story of one of these fools, who, through the issue of a very foolish deed, got for his wife the daughter of a king and became a wise man himself into the bargain.

In the Ligurian Sea there is an island called Capraia, which, at the time I am describing, was ruled by King Luciano. Amongst his subjects was a poor widow named Isotta, who lived with her only son Peter, a fisher-lad, but from Peter's fishing she would scarce have kept body and soul together, for he was a poor silly creature known to all the neighbours as Peter the Fool. Though he went fishing every day he never caught anything, but in spite of his ill-success he would always come up from his boat shouting and bellowing so that all the town might hear him: 'Mother, mother, bring out your tubs and your buckets and your pails; bring them out all, great and small, for Peter has caught a boatful of fish.' The poor woman soon got to know the value of Peter's bragging, but in spite of this she always prepared the vessels, only to find herself jeered at by the silly youth, who, as soon as he came near, would thrust out his long tongue in ridicule, and otherwise mock at her.

Now it chanced that the widow's cottage stood just opposite to the palace of King Luciano, who had only one child, a pretty graceful girl about ten years old, Luciana by name. She, it happened, was looking out of the window of the palace one day when Peter came back from fishing, crying out to his mother to bring out her tubs and her buckets and her pails to hold the fish with which he was laden, and so much was she diverted at the silly antics of the fool, that it seemed likely she would die with laughing. Peter, when he saw that he was made sport of, grew very angry, and threw some ugly words at her, but the more he raged the more she — after the manner of wilful children — laughed and made mock at him. Peter, however, went on with his fishing day after day, and played the same trick on his mother every evening on his return; but at last fortune favoured him, and he caught a fine tunny, very big and fat. Overjoyed at his good luck, he began to shout and cry out over and over again, 'Mother and I will have a good supper to-night,' when, to his amazement, he heard the tunny which he had just caught begin to speak: 'Ah! my dear brother, I pray you of your courtesy to give me my life. When once you have eaten me, what farther benefit do you think you will get from mė? but if you will let me live there is no telling what service I may not render you.' But Peter, whose thoughts just then were set only on his supper, hoisted the fish on his shoulders and set off homewards; but the tunny still kept on beseeching his captor to spare his life, promising him first as many fish as he could want, and finally to do him any favour he might demand. Peter was not hard-hearted, and, though a fool, fancied he might profit by sparing the fish, so he listened to the tunny's petition and threw him back into the sea. The fish, sensible of Peter's kindness, and not wishing to seem ungrateful, told Peter to get into his boat again and tilt it over so that the water could run in. This advice Peter at once followed, and, having leant over on one side, he let the boat be half filled with water, which brought in with it such a huge quantity of fish that the boat was in danger of sinking. Peter was wellnigh beside himself with joy when he saw what had happened, and, when he had taken as many fish as he could carry, he betook himself homewards, crying out, as was his wont, when he drew near to the cottage: 'Mother, mother, bring out your tubs and your buckets and your pails; bring out them all, great and small, for Peter has caught a boatful of fish.' At first poor Isotta, thinking that he was only playing his old fool's game, took no heed; but at last, hearing him cry out louder than ever, and fearing that he might commit some greater folly if he should not find the vessels prepared as usual, got them all ready. What was her surprise to see her simpleton of a son at last coming back with a brave spoil! The Princess Luciana was at the palace window, and hearing Peter bellowing louder than ever, she laughed louder than ever, so that Peter was almost mad with rage, and having left his fish, he rushed back to the seashore, and called aloud on the tunny to come and help him. The fish, hearing Peter's voice, came to the marge of the shore, and putting his nose up out of the waves, asked what service was required of him. 'What service!' cried Peter. 'Why I would that Luciana, that saucy minx, the daughter of our king, should find herself with child at once.'

What followed was a proof that the tunny had not made an empty promise to Peter, for before many days had passed the figure of the young girl, who was not twelve years old, began to show signs of maternity. Her mother, when she marked this, fell into great trouble, but she could not believe that a child of eleven could be pregnant, and rather set down the swelling to the working of an incurable disease; so she brought Luciana to be examined by some women expert in such cases, and these, as soon as they saw the girl, declared that she was certainly with child. The queen, overwhelmed by this terrible news, told it also to the king, and he, when he heard it, cried aloud for death rather than such ignominy. Strict inquisition was made to discover who could have violated the child, but nothing was found out; so Luciano, to hide her dire disgrace, determined to have his daughter secretly killed.

The queen, on hearing this, begged her husband to spare the unfortunate Luciana till the child should be born, and then do with her what he would. The king, moved with compassion for his only daughter, gave way so far; and in due time Luciana was delivered of a boy so fine and beautiful that the king could no longer harbour the thought of putting them away, but, on the other hand, gave order to the queen that the boy should be well tended till he was a year old. When this time was completed the child had become beautiful beyond compare, and then it came into the king's mind that he would again make a trial to find out who the father might be. He issued a proclamation that every man in the city who had passed fourteen years should, under pain of losing his head, present himself at the palace bearing in his hand some fruit or flower which might attract the child's attention. On the appointed day, in obedience to the proclamation, all those summoned came to the palace, bearing, this man one thing and that man another, and, having passed before the king, sat down according to their rank.

Now it happened that a certain young man as he was betaking himself to the palace met Peter, and said to him, 'Peter, why are you not going to the palace like all the others to obey the order of the king?' 'What should I do in such a crowd as that?' said Peter. 'Cannot you see I am a poor naked fellow, and have hardly a rag to my back, and yet you ask me to push myself in amongst all those gentlemen and courtiers? No.' Then the young man, laughing at him, said, 'Come with me, and I will give you a coat. Who knows whether the child may not turn out to be yours?' In the end Peter let himself be persuaded to go to the young man's house, and having put on a decent coat, they went together to the palace; but when they arrived there Peter's heart again failed him, and he hid himself behind a door. By this time all the men had presented themselves to the king, and were seated in the hall. Then Luciano commanded the nurse to bring in the child, thinking that if the father should be there the sense of paternity would make him give some sign. As the nurse carried the child down the hall everyone, as he passed, began to caress him and to give him, this one a fruit and that one a flower; but the infant, with a wave of his hand, refused them all. When the nurse passed by the entrance door the child began to laugh and crow, and threw himself forward so lustily that he almost jumped out of the woman's arms, but she, not knowing that anyone was there, walked on down the hall. When she came back to the same place, the child was more delighted than ever, laughing and pointing with his finger to the door; so that the king, who had already noticed the child's actions, called to the nurse, and asked her who was behind the door. The nurse, being somewhat confused, said that surely some beggar must be hidden there. By the king's command Peter was at once haled forth, and everybody recognized the town fool; but the child, who was close to him, stretched out his arms and clasped Peter round the neck, and kissed him lovingly. The king, recognizing the sign, was stricken to the heart with grief, and having discharged the assembly, commanded that Peter and Luciana and the child should be put to death forthwith.

The queen, though assenting to this doom, was fearful lest the public execution of the victims might draw down upon the king the anger of the people; so she persuaded him to have made a huge cask into which the three might be put and cast into the sea to drift at random; then, at least, no one might witness their dying agony. This the king agreed to; and when the cask was made, the condemned ones were put therein, with a basket of bread and a flask of wine, and a drum of figs for the child, and thrust out into the rough sea, with the expectation that the waves would soon dash it to pieces against the rocks; but this was not to be their fate.

Peter's poor old mother, when she heard of her son's misfortune, died of grief in a few days; and the unhappy Luciana, tossed about by the cruel waves, and seeing neither sun nor moon, would have welcomed a similar fate. The child, since she had no milk to give it, had to be soothed to sleep with now and then a fig; but Peter seemed to care for nothing, and ate the bread and drank the wine steadily, laughing the while. 'Alas! alas!' cried Luciana in despair, 'you care nothing for this evil which you have brought upon me, a poor innocent girl. You eat and drink and laugh without a thought of the danger around us.' 'Why,' replied Peter, 'this misfortune is more your own fault than mine. If you had not mocked me so, it would never have happened; but do not lose heart, our troubles will soon be over.' 'I believe that,' cried Luciana, 'for the cask will soon be split on a rock, and then we must all be drowned.' 'No, no,' said Peter, 'calm yourself. I have a secret, and were you to know what it is, you would be vastly surprised and vastly delighted too, I believe.' 'What secret can you know,' said Luciana, 'which will avail us in such danger as this?' 'I will soon tell you,' Peter replied. 'I have a faithful servant, a great fish, who will do me any service I ask of him, and there is nothing he cannot do. I may as well tell you it was through his working that you became with child.' 'That I cannot believe,' said Luciana; 'and what may this fish of yours be called?' 'His name is Signor Tunny,' replied Peter. 'Then,' said Luciana, 'to put your fish to the test, I will ask you to transfer to me the power you exercise over him, and to command him to do my bidding instead of yours.' 'Be it as you will,' said Peter; and without more ado he called the tunny, who at once rose up near the cask, whereupon Peter commanded him to do everything that Luciana might require of him. She at once exercised her power over the fish by ordering him to make the waves cast the cask ashore in a fair safe cleft in the rocks on an island, a short sail from her father's kingdom. As soon as the fish had worked her will so far, she laid other and much harder tasks upon him: one was to change Peter from the ugly fool that he was into a clever, handsome gallant; another was, to have built for her forthwith a rich and sumptuous palace, with lofty halls and chambers, and girt with carven terraces. Within the court there was to be laid out a beautiful garden, full of trees which should bear, instead of fruit, pearls and precious stones, and in the midst of it two fountains, one of the freshest water and the other of the finest wine. All these wonders were wrought by the fish almost as soon as Luciana had spoken.

Now all this time the king and the queen were in deep misery in thinking of the cruel death they had contrived for Luciana and her child, how they had given their own flesh and blood to be eaten by the fishes; therefore, to find some solace in their woe, they determined to go to Jerusalem and to visit the Holy Land. So they ordered a ship to be put in order for them, and furnished with all things suited to their state. They set sail with a favouring wind, and before they had gone a hundred miles they came in sight of an island upon which they could see a stately palace, built a little above the level of the sea. Seeing that this palace was so fair and sumptuous, and standing, moreover, within Luciano's kingdom, they were seized with a longing to view it more closely; so, having put into a haven, they landed on the island. Before they had come to the palace Luciana and Peter saw and recognized them, and, having gone forth to meet them, greeted them with a cordial welcome, but the king and queen did not know their hosts for the great change which had come over them. The guests were taken first into the palace, which they examined in every part, praising loudly its great beauty, and then they were led by a secret staircase into the garden, the splendour of which pleased them so amazingly that they swore they had never at any time before looked upon a place so delightful. In the centre of this garden there stood a noble tree, which bore on one of its branches three golden apples. These the keeper of the garden was charged to guard jealously against robbers, and now, by some secret working which I cannot unravel, the finest of these apples was transported into the folds of the king's robe about his bosom, and there hidden. Luciano and the queen were about to take their leave when the keeper approached and said to Luciana, 'Madam, the most beautiful of the three golden apples is missing, and I can find no trace of the thief.'

Luciana forthwith gave orders that the whole household should be searched, one by one, for such a loss as this was no light matter. The keeper, after he had searched thoroughly everyone, came back and told Luciana that the apple was nowhere to be found. At these words Luciana fell into great confusion, and, turning to the king, said: 'Your majesty must not be wroth with me if I ask that even you allow yourself to be searched, for I prize the golden apple that is lost almost as highly as my life.' The king, unsuspicious of any trick, and sure of his innocence, straightway loosened his robe, and lo! the golden apple fell from it to the ground.

The king stood as one dazed, ignorant as to how the golden apple could have come into his robe, and Luciana spoke: 'Sire, we have welcomed you to our house with all the worship fitting to your rank, and now, as a recompense, you would privily rob our garden of its finest fruit. Meseems you have proved yourself very ungrateful.' The king, in his innocence, attempted to prove to her that he could not have taken the apple, and Luciana, seeing his confusion, knew that the time had come for her to speak, and reveal herself to her father. 'My lord,' she said, with the tears in her eyes, 'I am Luciana, your hapless daughter, whom you sentenced to a cruel death along with my child and Peter the fisher-boy. Though I bore a child, I was never unchaste. Here is the boy, and here is he whom men were wont to call Peter the Fool. You wonder at this change. It has all been brought about by the power of a marvellous fish whose life Peter spared when he had caught it in his net. By this power Peter has been turned into the wisest of men, and the palace you see has been built. In the same way I became pregnant without knowledge of a man, and the golden apple was conveyed into the folds of your robe. I am as innocent of unchastity as you are of theft.'

When the king heard these words his eyes were opened, and he knew his child. Then, weeping with joy, they embraced each other, and all were glad and happy. After spending a few days on the island, they all embarked and returned together to Capraia, where with sumptuous feastings and rejoicings Peter was duly married to Luciana, and lived with her in great honour and contentment, until Luciano died, and then he became king in his stead.

The story of Cateruzza had at one time moved the ladies to tears; but, when its happy issue was made known to them, they rejoiced and thanked God therefor. Then the Signora, when Cateruzza had ended, commanded her to continue in the order they had followed hitherto, and she, not willing to hold in suspense the attention of her hearers, smilingly proposed to them the following enigma:

> Sir Redman stands behind a tree,
> Now hidden, now in sight is he.
> To him four runners speed along,
> Bearing a warrior huge and strong.
> Two darts into the trunk he wings,
> And Redman from his lair upsprings,
> And smites him from behind with skill;
> Thus ten little men one giant kill.
> Now he who shall this speech unfold,
> Shall be a witty rogue and bold.

Cateruzza's graceful and ingenious enigma was received by the whole company with applause. Many interpretations were put forth; but none came so near the mark as Lauretta: "Our sister's enigma can have but one meaning — the wild bull of the forest," she said. "He has four runners to carry his huge bulk. The sight of a red rag maddens him, and thinking to rend it, he strikes his horns into the tree. Straightway the huntsman, who was hidden behind the trunk, comes forth and kills him with a dart sped by ten little men, that is, the ten fingers of his two hands."

This speedy solution of her riddle raised an angry humour in Cateruzza's heart, for she had hoped it might prove beyond the wit of any; but she had not reckoned for Lauretta's quickness. The Signora, who perceived that the two were fain to wrangle, called for silence, and gave the word to Arianna to begin a story which should please them all, and the damsel, somewhat bashful, began as follows:

THE SECOND FABLE.

Dalfreno, King of Tunis, had two sons, one called Listico and the other Livoretto. The latter afterwards was known as Porcarollo, and in the end won for his wife Bellisandra, the daughter of Attarante, King of Damascus.

IT is no light matter for the steersman, let him be ever so watchful, to bring his tempest-strained bark safely into a sheltered port when he may be vexed by envious and contrary fortune, and tossed about amongst the hard and ragged rocks. And so it happened to Livoretto, son of the great King of Tunis, who, after many dangers hardly to be believed, heavy afflictions, and lengthened fatigues, succeeded at last, through the valour of his spirit, in trampling under foot his wretched fortune, and in the end reigned peacefully over his kingdom in Cairo. All this I shall make abundantly clear in the fable I am about to relate to you.

In Tunis, a stately city on the coast of Africa, there reigned, not long ago, a famous and powerful king named Dalfreno. He had to wife a beautiful and wise lady, and by her begot two sons, modest, well-doing and obedient in everything to their father, the elder being named Listico, and the younger Livoretto. Now it happened that by royal decree, as well as by the approved usage of the state, these youths were barred in the succession to their father's throne, which ran entirely in the female line. Wherefore the king, when he saw that he was by evil fortune deprived of female issue, and was assured by knowledge of himself that he was come to an age when he could hardly expect any further progeny, was sorely troubled, and felt his heart wrung thereanent with unbounded grief. And his sorrow was all the heavier because he was haunted by the dread that after his death his sons might be looked at askance, and evilly treated, and driven with ignominy from his kingdom.

The unhappy king, infected by these dolorous humours, and knowing not where might lie any remedy therefor, turned to the queen, whom he loved very dearly, and thus addressed her: 'Madam, what shall we do with these sons of ours, seeing that we are bereft of all power to leave them heirs to our kingdom both by the law and by the ancient custom of the land?' The sagacious queen at once made answer to him in these words: 'Sire, it seems to me that, as you have a greater store of riches than any other king in the world, you should send them away into some foreign country where no man would know them, giving them first a great quantity of money and jewels. In such case they may well find favour in the sight of some well-disposed sovereign, who will see that no ill befall them. And if (which may God forbid) they should happen to come to want, no one will know whose sons they are. They are young, fair to look upon, of good address, high-spirited, and on the alert for every honourable and knightly enterprise, and let them go where they will they will scarcely find any king or prince or great lord who will not love them and set great store upon them for the sake of the rich gifts which nature has lavished upon them.' This answer of the prudent queen accorded fully with the humour of King Dalfreno, and having summoned into his presence his sons Listico and Livoretto, he said to them: 'My well-beloved sons, you must by this time know that, after I am dead, you will have no chance of succeeding to the sovereignty of this my kingdom; not, indeed, on account of your vices or from your ill manner of living, but because it has been thus determined by law and by the ancient custom of the country. You being men, created by mother nature and ourselves, and not women, are barred from all claim. Wherefore your mother and I, for the benefit and advantage of you both, have determined to let you voyage into some strange land, taking with you jewels and gems and money in plenty; so that whenever you may light upon some honourable position you may gain your living in honourable wise, and do credit to us at the same time. And for this reason I look that you shall show yourselves obedient to our wishes.'

Listico and Livoretto were as much pleased at this proposition as the king and the queen themselves had been, because both one and other of the young men desired ardently to see new lands and to taste the pleasures of the world. It happened that the queen (as is not seldom the way with mothers) loved the younger son more tenderly than she loved the elder, and before they took their departure she called him aside and gave him a prancing high-mettled horse, flecked with spots, with a small shapely head, and high courage shining in its eye. Moreover, in addition to all these good qualities with which it was endowed, it was gifted with magic powers, but this last fact the queen told only to Livoretto, her younger son.

As soon, then, as the two sons had received their parents' benediction, and secured the treasure prepared for them, they departed secretly together; and after they had ridden for many days without lighting upon any spot which pleased them, they began to be sorely troubled at their fate. Then Livoretto spoke and addressed his brother: 'We have all this time ridden in one another's company, and narrowly searched the country without having wrought any deed which could add aught to our repute. Wherefore it seems to me wiser (supposing what I propose contents you also) that we should separate one from the other, and that each one should go in search of adventures for himself.'

Listico, having taken thought of his brother's proposition, agreed thereto, and then, after they had warmly embraced and kissed each other, they bade farewell and went their several ways. Listico, of whom nothing more was ever heard, took his way towards the West, while Livoretto journeyed into the East. And it happened that, after he had consumed a great space of time in going from one place to another, and seen almost every country under the sun, and spent all the jewels and the money and the other treasures his good father had given him, save and except the magic horse, Livoretto found himself at last in Cairo, the royal city of Egypt, which was at that time under the rule of a sultan whose name was Danebruno, a man wise in all the secrets of statecraft, and powerful through his riches and his high estate, but now heavily stricken in years. But, notwithstanding his advanced age, he was inflamed with the most ardent love for Bellisandra, the youthful daughter of Attarante, the King of Damascus, against which city he had at this time sent a powerful army with orders to camp round about it, and to lay siege to it, and to take it by storm, in order that, either by love or by force, he might win for himself the princess to wife. But Bellisandra, who had already a certain foreknowledge that the Sultan of Cairo was both old and ugly, had made up her mind once for all that, rather than be forced to become the wife of such a man, she would die by her own hand.

As soon as Livoretto had arrived at Cairo, and had gone into the city, and wandered into every part thereof, and marvelled at all he saw, he felt this was a place to his taste, and seeing that he had by this time lavished all his substance in paying for his maintenance, he determined that he would not depart thence until he should have taken service with some master or other. And one day, when he found himself by the palace of the sultan, he espied in the court thereof a great number of guards and mamelukes and slaves, and he questioned some of these as to whether there was in the court of the sultan lack of servants of any sort, and they answered him there was none. But, after a little, one of these, calling to mind that there was room in the household for a man to tend the pigs, shouted after him, and questioned him whether he would be willing to be a swineherd, and Livoretto answered 'Yes.' Then the man bade him get off his horse, and took him to the pigsties, asking at the same time what was his name. Livoretto told him, but hereafter men always called him Porcarollo, the name they gave him.

And thus it happened that Livoretto, now known by the name of Porcarollo, settled himself in the court of the sultan, and had no other employ than to let fatten the pigs, and in this duty he showed such great care and diligence that he brought to an end easily in two months tasks which would have taken any other man six months to accomplish. When, therefore, the guards and the mamelukes and the slaves perceived what a serviceable fellow he was, they persuaded the sultan that it would be well to provide some other employment for him, because his diligence and cleverness deserved some better office than the low one he now held. Wherefore, by the decree of the sultan, he was put in charge of all the horses in the royal stables, with a large augmentation of his salary, a promotion which pleased him mightily, because he deemed that, when he should be the master of all the other horses, he would be the better able to see well to his own. And when he got to work in his new office he cleaned and trimmed the horses so thoroughly, and made such good use of the currycomb, that their skins shone like satin.

Now, amongst the other horses there was an exceedingly beautiful high-spirited young palfrey, to which, on account of its good looks, he paid special attention in order to train it perfectly, and he trained it so well that the palfrey, besides going anywhere he might be told to go, would curve his neck, and dance, and stand at his whole height on his hind legs and paw the air so rapidly that every motion seemed like the flight of a bolt from a crossbow. The mamelukes and slaves, when they saw what Livoretto had taught the palfrey to do by his training, were thunderstruck with amazement, for it seemed to them that such things could hardly ensue in the course of nature. Wherefore they determined to tell the whole matter to the sultan, in order that he might take pleasure in witnessing the marvellous skill of Porcarollo.

The sultan, who always wore an appearance of great melancholy, whether from the torture of his amorous passion or by reason of his great age, cared little or nothing for recreation of any sort; but, weighed down by his troublesome humours, would pass the time in thinking of nothing else besides his beloved mistress. However, the mamelukes and the slaves made so much ado about the matter, that before long the sultan was moved to take his stand at the window one morning, and there to witness all the various wonderful and dexterous feats of horsemanship which Porcarollo performed with his trained palfrey, and, seeing what a good-looking youth he was, and how well formed in his person, and finding, moreover, that what he had seen was even more attractive than he had been led to expect, he came to the conclusion that it was mighty ill management (which now he began greatly to regret) to have sent so accomplished a youth to no better office than the feeding and tending of beasts. Wherefore, having turned the matter over in his mind, and considered it in every light, he realized to the full the eminent qualities, hitherto concealed, of the graceful young man, and found there was nothing lacking in him. So he resolved at once to remove him from the office he now filled, and to place him in one of higher consideration; so, having caused Porcarollo to be summoned into his presence, he thus addressed him: 'Porcarollo, it is my will that you do service no longer in the stables, as heretofore, but that you attend me at my own table and do the office of cupbearer, and taste everything that may be put before me, as a guarantee that I may eat thereof without hurt.'

The young man, after he had duly entered upon the office of cupbearer to the sultan, discharged his duties with so great art and skilfulness that he won the approbation, not only of the sultan, but of all those about the court. But amongst the mamelukes and slaves there arose against him such a bitter hatred and envy on account of the great favour done to him by the sultan that they could scarce bear the sight of him, and, had they not been kept back by the fear of their master, they would assuredly have taken his life. Therefore, in order to deprive the unfortunate youth of the favour of the sultan, and to let him either be slain or driven into perpetual exile, they devised a most cunning and ingenious plot for the furtherance of their design. They made beginning in this wise. One morning a slave named Chebur, who had been sent in his turn to do service to the sultan, said, 'My lord, I have some good news to give you.' 'And what may this be?' inquired the sultan. 'It is,' replied the slave, 'that Porcarollo, who bears by right the name of Livoretto, has been boasting that he would be able to accomplish for you even so heavy a task as to give into your keeping the daughter of Attarante, King of Damascus.' 'And how can such a thing as this be possible?' asked the sultan. To whom Chebur replied, 'It is indeed possible, O my lord! but if you will not put faith in my words, inquire of the mamelukes and of the other slaves, in whose presence he has boasted more than once of his power to do this thing, and then you will easily know whether the tale I am telling you be false or true.'

After the sultan had duly assured himself that what the slave had told to him was just, he summoned Liveretto into his presence, and demanded of him whether this saying concerning him which was openly bruited about the court, was true. Then the young man, who knew nothing of what had gone before, gave a stout denial, and spake so bluntly that the sultan, with his rage and animosity fully aroused, thus addressed him: 'Get you hence straightway, and if within the space of thirty days you have not brought into my power the Princess Bellisandra, the daughter of Attarante, King of Damascus, I will have your head taken off your shoulders.' The young man, when he heard this cruel speech of the sultan, withdrew from the presence overwhelmed with grief and confusion, and betook himself to the stables.

As soon as he had entered, the fairy horse, who remarked at once the sad looks of his master and the scalding tears which fell so plentifully from his eyes, turned to him and said: 'Alas! my master, why do I see you so deeply agitated and so full of grief?' The young man, weeping and sighing deeply the while, told him from beginning to end all that the sultan had required him to perform. Whereupon the horse, tossing his head and making signs as if he were laughing, managed to comfort him somewhat, and went on to bid him be of good heart and fear not, for all his affairs would come to a prosperous issue in the end. Then he said to his master: 'Go back to the sultan and beg him to give you a letter patent addressed to the captain-general of his army who is now laying siege to Damascus, in which letter he shall write to the general an express command that, as soon as he shall have seen and read the letter patent sealed with the sultan's great seal, he shall forthwith raise the siege of the city, and give to you money and fine clothing and arms in order that you may be able to prosecute with vigour and spirit the great enterprise which lies before you. And if peradventure it should happen, during your voyage thitherward, that any person or any animal of whatever sort or condition should entreat you to do them service of any kind, take heed that you perform the favour which may be required of you, nor, as you hold your life dear to you, refuse to do the service asked for. And if you should meet with any man who is anxious to purchase me of you, tell him that you are willing to sell me, but at the same time demand for me a price so extravagant that he shall give up all thought of the bargain. But if at any time a woman should wish to buy me, bear yourself gently towards her, and do her every possible courtesy, giving her full liberty to stroke my head, my forehead, my eyes and ears, and my loins, and to do anything else she may have a mind to, for I will let them handle me as they will without doing them the least mischief or hurt of any kind.'

When he heard these words the young man, full of hope and spirit, went back to the sultan and made a request to him for the letter patent and for everything else that the fairy horse had named to him. And when he had procured all these from the sultan, he straightway mounted the horse and took the road which led to Damascus, giving by his departure great delight to all the mamelukes and slaves, who, on account of the burning envy and unspeakable hate they harboured against him, held it for certain that he would never again come back alive to Cairo. Now it happened that, when Livoretto had been a long time on his journey, he came one day to a pool, and he marked, as he passed by the end thereof, that the shore gave forth a very offensive smell, the cause of which I cannot tell, so that one could hardly go near to the place, and there upon the shore he saw lying a fish half dead. The fish, when it saw Livoretto approaching, cried out: 'Alas! kind gentleman, I beseech you of your courtesy to set me free from this foul-smelling mud, for I am, as you may see, wellnigh dead on account of it. The young man, taking good heed of all that the fairy horse had told him, forthwith got down from his saddle and drew the fish out of the ill-smelling water, and washed it clean with his own hands. Then the fish, after it had returned due thanks to Livoretto for the kindness he had done for it, said to him: 'Take from my back the three biggest scales you can find, and keep them carefully by you; and if at any time it shall happen that you are in need of succour, put down the scales by the bank of the river, and I will come to you straightway and will give you instant help.'

Livoretto accordingly took the three scales, and, having thrown the fish, which was now quite clean and shining, into the clear water, remounted his horse and rode on until he came to a certain place where he found a peregrine falcon which had been frozen into a sheet of ice as far as the middle of its body, and could not get free. The falcon, when it saw the young man, cried out: 'Alas! fair youth, take pity on me, and release me from this ice in which, as you see, I am imprisoned, and I promise, if you will deliver me from this great misfortune, I will lend you my aid if at any time you should chance to stand in need thereof.' The young man, overcome by compassion and pity, went kindly to the succour of the bird, and having drawn a knife which he carried attached to the scabbard of his sword, he beat and pierced with the point thereof the hard ice round about the bird so that he brake it, and then he took out the falcon and cherished it in his bosom in order to bring back somewhat of warmth to its body. The falcon, when it had recovered its strength and was itself again, thanked the young man profusely for his kindness, and as a recompense for the great service he had wrought, it gave him two feathers which he would find growing under its left wing, begging him at the same time to guard and preserve them most carefully for the sake of the love it bore him; for if in the future he should chance to stand in need of any succour, he might take the two feathers to the river and stick them in the bank there, and then immediately it would come to his assistance. And having thus spoken the bird flew away.

After Livoretto had continued his journey for some days he came to the sultan's army encamped before the city, and there he found the captain-general, who was vexing the place with fierce assaults. Having been brought into the general's presence, he drew forth the sultan's letter patent, and the general, as soon as he had mastered the contents thereof, immediately gave orders that the siege should be raised, and this having been done he marched back to Cairo with his whole army. Livoretto, after watching the departure of the captain-general, made his way the next morning into the city of Damascus by himself, and having taken up his quarters at an inn, he attired himself in a very fair and rich garment, all covered with most rare and precious gems, which shone bright enough to make the sun envious, and mounted his fairy horse, and rode into the piazza in front of the royal palace, where he made the horse go through all the exercises he had taught it with so great readiness and dexterity, that everyone who beheld him stood still in amazement and could look at nought beside.

Now it happened that the noise made by the tumultuous crowd in the piazza below roused from sleep the Princess Bellisandra, and she forthwith arose from her bed. Having gone out upon a balcony, which commanded a view of all the square beneath, she saw there a very handsome youth; but what she marked especially was the beauty and vivacity of the gallant and high-mettled horse on which he sat. In short, she was seized with a desire to get this horse for her own, just as keen as the passion of an amorous youth for the fair maiden on whom he has set his heart. So she went at once to her father and besought him most urgently to buy the horse for her, because ever since she had looked upon his beauty and grace she had come to feel that she could not live without him. Then the king, for the gratification of the fancy of his daughter, whom he loved very tenderly, sent out one of his chief nobles to ask Livoretto whether he would be willing to sell his horse for any reasonable price, because the only daughter of the king was taken with the keenest desire to possess it. On hearing this Livoretto answered that there was nothing on earth precious and excellent enough to be accounted as a price for the horse, and demanded therefor a greater sum of money than there was in all the dominions which the king had inherited from his fathers. When the king heard the enormous price asked by Livoretto, he called his daughter and said to her: 'My daughter, I cannot bring myself to lavish the value of my whole kingdom in purchasing for you this horse and in satisfying your desire. Wherefore have a little patience, and live happy and contented, for I will make search and buy you another horse even better and more beautiful than this.'

But the effect of these words of the king was to inflame Bellisandra with yet more ardent longing to possess the horse, and she besought her father more insistently than ever to buy it for her, no matter how great might be the price he had to pay for it. Then the maiden, after much praying and intercession, found that her entreaties had no avail with her father, so she left him, and betook herself to her mother, and feigning to be half dead and prostrate with despair, fell into her arms. The mother, filled with pity, and seeing her child so deeply grief-stricken and pale, gave her what gentle consolation she could, and begged her to moderate her grief, and suggested that, as soon as the king should be out of the way, they two should seek out the young man and should bargain with him for the purchase of the horse, and then perhaps (because they were women) he would let them have it at a more reasonable price. The maiden, when she heard these kindly words of her beloved mother, was somewhat comforted, and as soon as the king was gone elsewhere the queen straightway despatched a messenger to Livoretto, bidding him to come at once to the palace and to bring his horse with him; and he, when he heard the message thus delivered to him, rejoiced greatly, and at once betook himself to the court. When he was come into the queen's presence, she forthwith asked him what price he demanded for the horse which her daughter so much desired to possess, and he answered her in these words: 'Madam, if you were to offer to give me all you possess in the world for my horse it could never become your daughter's as a purchase, but if it should please her to accept it as a gift, she can have it for nothing. Before she takes it as a present, however, I had rather that she should make trial of it, for it is so gentle and well-trained that it will allow anybody to mount it without difficulty.' With these words he got down from the saddle and helped the princess to mount therein; whereupon she, holding the reins in her hand, made it go here and there and managed it perfectly. But after a little, when the princess had gone on the horse about a stone's throw distant from her mother, Livoretto sprang suddenly upon the crupper of the horse, and struck his spurs deep into the flanks of the beast, and pricked it so sharply that it went as quickly as if it had been a bird flying through the air. The maiden, bewildered at this strange conduct, began to cry out: 'You wicked and disloyal traitor! Whither are you carrying me, you dog, and son of a dog?' However, all her cries and reproaches were to no purpose, for there was no one near to give her aid or even to comfort her with a word.

It happened as they rode along that they came to the bank of a river, and in passing this the maiden drew off from her finger a very beautiful ring which she wore thereon, and cast it secretly into the water. And after they had been for many days on their journey, they arrived at last at Cairo, and as soon as Livoretto had come to the palace he immediately took the princess and presented her to the sultan, who, when he saw how lovely and graceful and pure she was, rejoiced greatly, and bade her welcome with all sorts of kindly speeches. And after a while, when the hour for retiring to rest had come, and the sultan had retired with the princess to a chamber as richly adorned as it was beautiful in itself, the princess spake thus to the sultan: 'Sire, do not dream that I will ever yield to your amorous wishes unless you first command that wicked and rascally servant of yours to find my ring which fell into the river as we journeyed hither. When he shall have recovered it and brought it back to me you will see that I shall be ready to comply with your desire.' The sultan, who was by this time all on fire with love for the deeply injured princess, could deny her nothing which might please her; so he turned to Livoretto and bade him straightway set forth in quest of the ring, threatening him that if he should fail in his task he should immediately be put to death.

Livoretto, as soon as he heard the words of the sultan, perceived that these were orders which must be carried out at once, and that he would put himself in great danger by running counter to his master's wishes; so he went out of his presence deeply troubled, and betook himself to the stables, where he wept long and bitterly, for he was altogether without hope that he would ever be able to recover the princess's ring. The fairy horse, when he saw his master thus heavily stricken with grief and weeping so piteously, asked him what evil could have come to him to make him shed such bitter tears; and after Livoretto had told him the cause thereof, the horse thus addressed his master: 'Ah, my poor master! cease, I pray you, to talk in this strain. Remember the words that the fish spake to you, and open your ears to hear what I shall say, and take good heed to carry out everything as I shall direct you. Go back to the sultan and ask him for all you may need for your enterprise, and then set about it with a confident spirit, and have no doubts.' Livoretto therefore did exactly what the horse commanded him to do, no more and no less; and, after having travelled for some time, came at last to that particular spot where he had crossed the river with the princess, and there he laid the three scales of the fish on the green turf of the bank. Whereupon the fish, gliding through the bright and limpid stream, leaping now to this side and now to that, swam up to where Livoretto stood with every manifestation of joy and gladness, and, having brought out of his mouth the rare and precious ring, he delivered it into Livoretto's hand, and when he had taken back his three scales he plunged beneath the water and disappeared.

As soon as Livoretto had got the ring safely back, all his sorrow at once gave place to gladness, and without any delay he took his way home to Cairo, and when he had come into the sultan's presence and had made formal obeisance to him, he presented the ring to the princess. The sultan, as soon as he saw that her wishes had been fulfilled by the restoration of the precious ring she had desired so ardently, began to court her with the most tender and amorous caresses and flattering speeches, hoping thereby to induce her to lie with him that night; but all his supplications and wooings were in vain, for the princess said to him: 'Sir, do not think to deceive me with your fine words and false speeches. I swear to you that you shall never take your pleasure of me until that ruffian, that false rascal who entrapped me with his horse and conveyed me hither, shall have brought me some of the water of life.' The sultan, who was anxious not to cross or contradict in any way this lady of whom he was so much enamoured, but did all in his power to please her, straightway summoned Livoretto, and bade him in a severe tone to go forth and to bring back with him some of the water of life, or to lose his head.

Livoretto, when he heard the impossible demand that was made upon him, was terribly overcome with grief; moreover, the wrath which was kindled in his heart burst out into a flame, and he complained bitterly that the sultan should offer him so wretched a return as this for all the faithful service he had given, and for all the heavy and prolonged fatigue he had undergone, putting his own life the while in the most imminent danger. But the sultan, burning with love, was in no mind to set aside the purpose he had formed for satisfying the wishes of the lady he loved so much, and let it be known that he would have the water of life found for her at any cost. So when Livoretto went out of his master's presence he betook himself, as was his wont, to the stables, cursing his evil fortune and weeping bitterly all the while. The horse, when he saw the heavy grief in which his master was, and listened to his bitter lamentations, spake to him thus: 'O my master! why do you torment yourself in this fashion? Tell me if any fresh ill has happened to you. Calm yourself as well as you can, and remember that a remedy is to be found for every evil under the sun, except for death.' And when the horse had heard the reason of Liveretto's bitter weeping, it comforted him with gentle words, bidding him recall to memory what had been spoken to him by the falcon which he had delivered from its frozen bonds of ice, and the valuable gift of the two feathers. Whereupon the unhappy Livoretto, having taken heed of all the horse said to him, mounted it and rode away. He carried with him a small phial of glass, well sealed at the mouth, and this he made fast to his girdle. Then he rode onward and onward till he came to the spot where he had set the falcon at liberty, and there he planted the two feathers in the bank of the river according to the direction he had received, and suddenly the falcon appeared in the air and asked him what his need might be. To this Livoretto answered that he wanted some of the water of life; and the falcon, when he heard these words, cried out, 'Alas, alas, gentle knight! the thing you seek is impossible. You will never get it by your own power, because the fountain from which it springs is always guarded and narrowly watched by two savage lions and by two dragons, who roar horribly day and night without ceasing, and mangle miserably and devour all those who would approach the fountain to take of the water. But now, as a recompense for the great service you once rendered me, take the phial which hangs at your side, and fasten it under my right wing, and see that you depart not from this place until I shall have returned.'

When Livoretto had done all this as the falcon had ordered, the bird rose up from the earth with the phial attached to its wing, and flew away to the region where was the fountain of the water of life, and, having secretly filled the phial with the water, returned to the place where Livoretto was, and gave to him the phial. Then he took up his two feathers and flew away out of sight.

Livoretto, in great joy that he had indeed procured some of the precious water, without making any more delay returned to Cairo in haste, and, having arrived there, he presented himself to the sultan, who was passing the time in pleasant converse with Bellisandra, his beloved lady. The sultan took the water of life, and in high glee gave it to the princess, and, as soon as she could call this precious fluid her own, he recommenced his entreaties that she would, according to her promise, yield herself to his pleasure. But she, firm as a strong tower beaten about by the raging winds, declared that she would never consent to gratify his desire unless he should first cut off with his own hands the head of that Livoretto who had been to her the cause of so great shame and disaster. When the sultan heard this savage demand of the cruel princess, he was in no degree moved to comply with it, because it seemed to him a most shameful thing that, as a recompense for all the great labours he had accomplished, Livoretto should be thus cruelly bereft of life. But the treacherous and wicked princess, resolutely determined to work her nefarious purpose, snatched up a naked dagger, and with all the daring and violence of a man struck the youth in the throat while the sultan was standing by, and, because there was no one present with courage enough to give succour to the unhappy Livoretto, he fell dead.

And not content with this cruel outrage, the bloody-minded girl hewed off his head from his shoulders, and, having chopped his flesh into small pieces, and torn up his nerves, and broken his hard bones and ground them to a fine powder, she took a large bowl of copper, and little by little she threw therein the pounded and cut-up flesh, compounding it with the bones and the nerves as women of a household are wont to do when they make a great pasty with a leavened crust thereto. And after all was well kneaded, and the cut-up flesh thoroughly blended with the powdered bones and the nerves, the princess fashioned out of the mixed-up mass the fine and shapely image of a man, and this she sprinkled with the water of life out of the phial, and straightway the young man was restored to life from death more handsome and more graceful than he had ever been before.

The sultan, who felt the weight of his years heavy upon him, no sooner saw this amazing feat and the great miracle which was wrought, than he was struck with astonishment and stood as one confounded. Then he felt a great longing to be made again a youth, so he begged Bellisandra to treat him in the same way as she had treated Livoretto. Then the princess, who tarried not a moment to obey this command of the sultan, took up the sharp knife which was still wet with Livoretto's blood, and, having seized him by the throat with her left hand, held him fast while she dealt him a mortal blow in the breast. Then she commanded the slaves to throw the body of the sultan out of the window into the deep ditch which ran round the walls of the palace, and thus, instead of being restored to youth as was Livoretto, he became food for dogs after the miserable end he made.

After she had wrought this terrible deed the Princess Bellisandra was greatly feared and reverenced by all in the city on account of the strange and marvellous power that was in her, and when the news was brought to her that the young man was a son of Dalfreno, King of Tunis, and that his rightful name was Livoretto, she wrote a letter to the old father, giving him therein a full account of all the amazing accidents which had befallen his son, and begging him most urgently to come at once to Cairo in order that he might be present at the nuptials of herself and Livoretto. And King Dalfreno, when he heard this good news about his son — of whom no word had been brought since he left Tunis with his brother — rejoiced greatly, and, having put all his affairs in good order, betook himself to Cairo and was welcomed by the whole city with the most distinguished marks of honour. After the space of a few days Bellisandra and Livoretto were married amidst the rejoicings of the whole people, and thus with the princess as his lawful spouse, with sumptuous triumphs and feastings, and with the happiest omens, Livoretto was made the Sultan of Cairo, where for many years he governed his realm in peace and lived a life of pleasure and tranquillity. Dalfreno tarried in Cairo a few days after the nuptials, and then took leave of his son and daughter-in-law and returned to Tunis safe and sound.

As soon as Arianna had come to the end of her interesting story, she propounded her enigma forthwith, in order that the rule which governed the entertainment might be strictly kept:

> Small what though my compass be,
> A mighty furnace gendered me.

The covering which round me clings,
Is what from marshy plains upsprings.
My soul, which should be free as air,
Is doomed a prisoner close to fare.
It is a liquor bland and sweet.
No jest is this which I repeat:
All silken are my festal clothes,
And man will put me to his nose,
To make me all my charms disclose.

All those assembled listened with the keenest attention to the ingenious enigma set forth by Arianna, and they made her repeat it over and over again, but not one of the whole company proved to have wit sharp enough for the disentangling thereof. At last the fair Arianna gave the solution in these words: "Ladies and gentlemen, my enigma is supposed to describe a little flask of rose water, which has a body of glass born in a fiery furnace. Its covering comes from the marshes, for it is made of straw, and the soul which is contained within is the rose water. The gown or robe with which it is surrounded is the vessel, and whosoever sees it puts it under his nose to enjoy the odour thereof."

As soon as Arianna had given the solution of her enigma, Lauretta, who was seated next to her, remembered that it was her turn to speak. Wherefore without waiting for any further command from the Signora she thus began.

THE THIRD FABLE.

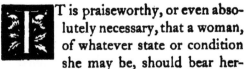

Biancabella, the daughter of Lamberico, Marquis of Monferrato, is sent away by the step-mother of Ferrandino, King of Naples, in order that she may be put to death; but the assassins only cut off her hands and put out her eyes. Afterwards she, her hurts having been healed by a snake, returns happily to Ferrandino.

IT is praiseworthy, or even absolutely necessary, that a woman, of whatever state or condition she may be, should bear herself with prudence in each and every undertaking she may essay, for without prudence nothing will bring itself to a commendable issue. And if a certain stepmother, of whom I am about to tell you, had used it with due moderation when she plotted wickedly to take another's life, she would not herself have been cut off by divine judgment in such fashion as I will now relate to you.

Once upon a time, now many years ago, there reigned in Monferrato a marquis called Lamberico, very puissant, both on account of his lordships and his great wealth, but wanting in children to carry on his name. He was, forsooth, mighty anxious for progeny, but this bounty of heaven was denied to him. Now one day it chanced that the marchioness his wife was walking for her pleasure in the palace garden, and, being suddenly overcome by sleep, she sat down at the foot of a tree and slumber fell upon her. While she slept gently there crept up to her side a very small snake, which, having passed stealthily under her clothes without arousing her by its presence, made its way into her body, and by subtle windings penetrated even into her womb, and there lay quiet. Before long time had elapsed the marchioness, with no small pleasure to herself, and with the highest delight of all the state, proved to be with child, and, when the season of her lying-in came, she was delivered of a female child, round the neck of which there was coiled three times something in the similitude of a serpent. When the midwives, who were in attendance upon the marchioness, saw this, they were much affrighted; but the snake, without causing any hurt whatsoever, untwined itself from the infant's neck, and, winding itself along the floor and stretching itself out, made its way into the garden.

Now when the child had been duly cared for and clothed, the nurses having washed it clean in a bath of clear water and swathed it in snow-white linen, they began to see, little by little, that round about its neck was a collar of gold, fashioned with the most subtle handiwork. So fine was it, and so lovely, that it seemed to shed its lustre from between the skin and the flesh, just as the most precious jewels are wont to shine out from a closure of transparent crystal, and, moreover, it encircled the neck of the infant just as many times as the little serpent had cast its fold thereabout. The little girl, to whom, on account of her exceeding loveliness, the name of Biancabella was given, grew up in such goodliness and beauty that it seemed as if she must be sprung from divine and not from human stock. When she had come to the age of ten years it chanced that one day she went with her nurse upon a terrace, from whence she observed a fair garden full of roses and all manner of other lovely flowers. Then, turning towards the nurse who had her in charge, she demanded of her what garden that was which she had never seen before. To this the nurse replied that it was a place which her mother called her own garden, and one, moreover, in which she was wont often to take her recreation. Then said the child to her: 'I have never seen anything so fair before, and I had fain go into it and walk there.' Then the nurse, taking Biancabella by the hand, led her into the garden, and, having suffered the child to go a little distance apart from her, she sat down under the shade of a leafy beech-tree and settled herself to sleep, letting the little girl take her pleasure the while in roaming about the garden. Biancabella, who was altogether charmed with the loveliness of the place, ran about, now here and now there, gathering flowers, and, at last, when she felt somewhat tired, she sat down under the shadow of a tree. Now scarcely had the child seated herself upon the ground when there appeared a little snake, which crept up close to her side. Biancabella, as soon as she saw the beast, was mightily alarmed, and was about to cry out, when the snake thus addressed her: 'Cry not, I beg you, neither disturb yourself, nor have any fear, for know that I am your sister, born on the same day as yourself and at the same birth, and that Samaritana is my name. And I now tell you that, if you will be obedient to what I shall command you, I will make you happy in your life; but if, on the other hand, you disobey me, you will come to be the most luckless, the most wretched woman the world has ever yet seen. Wherefore, go your way now, without fear of any sort, and to-morrow cause to be brought into this garden two vessels, of which let one be filled with pure milk, and the other with the finest water of roses. Then you must come to me by yourself without companions.'

When the serpent was gone the little girl rose up from her seat and went back to seek her nurse, whom she found still sleeping, and, having aroused her, she returned with her to the palace without saying aught of what had befallen her.

And when the morrow had come Biancabella chanced to be with her mother alone in the chamber, and the mother remarked that the child bore upon her face a melancholy look. Whereupon she said: 'Biancabella, what ails you that you put on so discontented a face? You are wont to be lively and merry enough, but now you seem all sad and woebegone.' To this Biancabella replied: 'There is nothing amiss with me; it is only that I want to have taken into the garden two vessels, of which one shall be filled with pure milk and the other of the finest water of roses.' The mother answered: 'And why do you let yourself be troubled by so small a matter as this, my child? Do you not know that everything here belongs to you?' Then the marchioness caused to be brought to her two vessels, large and beautiful, filled, the one with milk and the other with rose water, and had them carried into the garden.

When the hour appointed by the

Biancabella And The Enchanted Serpent
Night the Third
THIRD FABLE

Biancabella And The Enchanted Serpent

Night the Third

THIRD FABLE

Biancabella And The Enchanted Serpent

Night the Third

THIRD FABLE

Biancabella And The Enchanted Serpent

Night the Third

THIRD FABLE

serpent had come, Biancabella, without taking any other damsel to bear her company, repaired to the garden, and, having opened the door thereof, she went in and made fast the entrance, and then seated herself upon the ground at the spot where the two vessels had been placed. Almost as soon as she had sat down the serpent appeared and came near her, and straightway commanded her to strip off all her clothes, and then, naked as she was, to step into the vessel which was filled with milk. When she had done this, the serpent twined itself about her, thus bathing her body in every part with the white milk and licking her all over with his tongue, rendering her pure and perfect in every part where, peradventure, aught that was faulty might have been found. Next, having bid her come out of the vessel of milk, the serpent made her enter the one which was filled with rose water, whereupon all her limbs were scented with odours so sweet and restorative that she felt as if she were filled with fresh life. Then the serpent bade her put on her clothes once more, giving her at the same time express command that she should hold her peace as to what had befallen her, and to speak no word thereanent even to her father and mother. For the serpent willed that no other woman in all the world should be found to equal Biancabella in beauty or in grace. And finally, after she had bestowed upon her every good quality, the serpent crept away to its hiding-place.

When this was done Biancabella left the garden and returned to the palace. Her mother, when she perceived how her daughter had become more lovely and gracious than ever, and fairer than any other damsel in the world, was astonished beyond measure and knew not what to say. Wherefore she questioned the young girl as to what she had done to indue herself with such surpassing loveliness; but Biancabella had no answer to give her. Hereupon the marchioness took a comb and began to comb and dress her daughter's fair locks, and forthwith from the girl's hair there fell down pearls and all manner of precious stones, and when Biancabella went to wash her hands roses and violets and lovely flowers of all sorts sprang up around them, and the odours which arose from these were so sweet that it seemed as if the place had indeed become an earthly paradise. Her mother, when she saw this marvel, ran to find Lamberico her husband, and, full of maternal pride, thus addressed him: 'My lord, heaven has bestowed upon us a daughter who is the sweetest, the loveliest, and the most exquisite work nature ever produced. For besides the divine beauty and grace in her, which is manifest to all eyes, pearls and gems and all other kinds of precious stones fall from her hair, and—to name something yet more marvellous—round about her white hands spring up roses and violets and all manner of flowers which give out the sweetest odours to all those who may come near her to wonder at the sight. All this I tell to you I assuredly would never have believed had I not looked thereon with my own eyes.'

Her husband, who was of an unbelieving nature, was at first disinclined to put faith in his wife's words, and treated her speech as a subject for laughter and ridicule, but she went on plying him without ceasing with accounts of what she had witnessed, so that he determined to see for himself how the matter really stood. Then, having made them bring his daughter into his presence, he found about her even more marvellous things than his wife had described, and on account of what he saw he rejoiced exceedingly, and in his pride swore a great oath that there was in the whole world no man worthy to be united to her in wedlock.

Very soon the fame and glory of the supreme and immortal beauty of Biancabella began to spread itself through the whole world, and many kings and princes and nobles came together from all parts in order to win her love and favour and have her to wife, but not one of all these suitors was counted worthy to enjoy her, inasmuch as each one of them proved to be lacking in respect of one thing or another. But at last one day there came a-wooing Ferrandino, King of Naples, who by his prowess and by his illustrious name blazed out resplendent like the sun in the midst of the smaller luminaries, and, having presented himself to the marquis, demanded of him the hand of his daughter in marriage. The marquis, seeing that the suitor was seemly of countenance, and well knit in person, and full of grace, besides being a prince of great power and possessions and wealth, gave his consent to the nuptials at once, and, having summoned his daughter, without further parleying the two were betrothed by joining of hands and by kissing one another.

Scarcely were the rites of betrothal completed, when Biancabella called back to mind the words which her sister Samaritana had so lovingly spoken to her, wherefore she withdrew herself from the presence of her spouse under the pretext that she had certain business of her own to see to, and, having gone to her own chamber, made fast the door thereof from within, and then passed by a secret thoroughfare into the garden. When she had come into the garden, she began to call upon Samaritana in a low voice. But the serpent no more manifested herself as heretofore, and Biancabella, when she perceived this, was mightily astonished, and, after she had searched through every part of the garden without finding a trace of Samaritana, a deep grief fell upon her, for she knew that this thing had happened to her because she had not given due attention and obedience to the commands which her sister had laid upon her. Wherefore, grieving and bewailing heavily on account of the mischance that had befallen her, she returned into her chamber, and having opened the door, she went to rejoin her spouse, who had been waiting a long time for her, and sat down beside him. When the marriage ceremonies were completed, Ferrandino led his bride away with him to Naples, where, with sumptuous state and magnificent festivities and the sound of trumpets, they were welcomed by the whole city with the highest honour.

It happened that there was living at Naples Ferrandino's stepmother, who had two daughters of her own, both of them deformed and ugly; but, notwithstanding this, she had set her heart on marrying one of them to the king. But now, when all hope was taken from her of ever accomplishing this design of hers, her rage and anger against Biancabella became so savage that she could scarcely endure to look upon her. But she was careful to conceal her animosity, feigning the while to hold Biancabella in all love and affection. Now by a certain freak of fortune the King of Tunis at this time began to set in array a mighty force of armed men for service by land and likewise on sea, in order that he might incite Ferrandino to make war (whether he did this because Ferrandino had won Biancabella to wife, or for some other reason I know not), and at the head of a very powerful army he had already passed the bounds of the kingdom of Naples. On this account it was necessary that Ferrandino should straightway take up arms for the defence of his realm, and hurry to the field to confront his foe. Therefore, having settled his affairs, and made provision of all things necessary for Biancabella (she being now with child), he gave her over to the care of his stepmother and set forth with his army.

Ferrandino had not long departed when this malevolent and froward-minded woman made a wicked design on Biancabella's life, and, having summoned into her presence certain retainers who were entirely devoted to her, she charged them to conduct Biancabella with them to some place or other — feigning that what they were doing was done for her recreation —and that they should not leave her until they had taken her life. Moreover, in order that she might be fully assured that they had discharged their duty, they were to bring back to her some sign of Biancabella's death. These ruffians, prompt for any sort of ill-doing, at once prepared to carry out the commands of their mistress, and making pretence of conducting Biancabella to some place where she might recreate herself, they carried her away into a wood, and forthwith began to make preparation to kill her. But when they perceived how lovely she was, and gracious, they were moved to pity and had not the heart to take her life. So they cut off both her hands and tore her eyes out of her head, and these they carried back to the stepmother as certain proofs that Biancabella had been killed by them. When this impious and cruel woman saw what they brought in their hands, her joy and satisfaction were unbounded, and, scheming still in her wicked heart to carry out her nefarious designs, she spread through all the kingdom a report that both her own daughters were dead, the one of a continued fever, and the other of an impostume of the heart, which had caused her death by suffocation. Moreover, she went on to declare that Biancabella, disordered by grief at the king's departure, had miscarried of a child, and had likewise been seized with a tertian fever which had wasted her so cruelly that there was more cause to fear her death than to hope for her recovery. But the scheme of this wicked cunning woman was to keep one of her own daughters in the king's bed, maintaining the while that she was Biancabella, shrunken and distempered by the fever.

Ferrandino, after he had attacked and put to rout the army of his foe, marched homeward in all the triumph of victory, hoping to find his beloved Biancabella full of joy and happiness, but in lieu of this he found her (as he believed) lying in bed shrivelled, pale, and disfigured. Then he went up to the bed and gazed closely at her face, and was overcome with astonishment when he looked upon the wreck she had become, and could hardly persuade himself that the woman he saw there could really be Biancabella. Afterwards he bade her attendants comb her hair, and, in place of the gems and the precious jewels which were wont to fall from the fair locks of his wife, there came forth great worms which had been feeding on the wretched woman's flesh, and from the hands there came forth, not the roses and the sweet-smelling flowers which ever sprang up around Biancabella's, but a foulness and filth which caused a nauseous sickness to all who came near her. But the wicked old stepmother kept on speaking words of consolation to him, declaring that all this distemper sprang from nothing else than the lengthened course of the ailment which possessed her.

In the meantime the ill-fated Biancabella, bereft of her hands and blind in both her eyes, was left alone in that solitary place, and, finding herself in such cruel affliction, she called over and over again upon her sister Samaritana, beseeching her to come to her rescue; but no answer came to her except from the resounding voice of Echo, who cried aloud through all the place. And while the unhappy Biancabella was left in the agony of despair, conscious that she was cut off from all human aid, there came into the wood a venerable old man, kindly of aspect and no less kindly in his heart. And he, when he listened to the sad and mournful voice which smote upon his hearing, made his way step by step towards the place whence it came, and stopped when he found there a blind lady with her hands cut off who was bitterly mourning the sad fate which had overtaken her. When the good old man looked upon her, and saw how sad was her condition, he could not bear to leave her thus in this wilderness of broken trees and thorns and brambles, but, overcome by the fatherly pity within him, he led her home with him to his house, and gave her into the charge of his wife, commanding her very strictly to take good care of the sufferer. Then he turned towards his three daughters, who verily were as beautiful as three of the brightest stars of heaven, and exhorted them earnestly to keep her company, and to render to her continually any loving service she might require, and to take care that she wanted for nothing. But the wife, who had a hard heart, and none of the old man's pity, was violently moved to anger by these words of her husband, and, turning towards him, cried out: 'Husband, what is this you would have us do with this woman, all blind and maimed as she is? Doubtless she has been thus treated as a punishment for her sins, and for no good behaviour.' In reply to this speech the old man spake in an angry tone: 'You will carry out all the commands I give you. If you should do aught else, you need not look to see me here again.'

It happened that while the unhappy Biancabella was left in charge of the wife and the three daughters, conversing with them of various things, and meditating over her own great misfortunes, she besought one of the maidens to do her a favour and comb her hair a little. But when the mother heard this she was much angered, forasmuch as she would not allow either of her children to minister in any way to the unfortunate sufferer. But the daughter's heart was more given to pity than was her mother's, and moreover she called to mind what her father's commands had been, and was conscious of some subtle air of dignity and high breeding which seemed to emanate from Biancabella as a token of her lofty estate. So she straightway unfastened the apron from her waist, and, having spread it on the floor beside Biancabella, began to comb her hair softly and carefully. Scarcely had she passed the comb thrice through the blond tresses before there fell out of them pearls and rubies and diamonds and all sorts of precious stones. Now the mother, when she saw what had happened, was seized with dread, and stood as one struck with amazement; moreover, the great dislike which at first she had harboured towards Biancabella, now gave way to a feeling of kindly affection. And when the old man had come back to the house they all ran to embrace him, rejoicing with him greatly over the stroke of good fortune which had come to deliver them from the bitter poverty which had hitherto oppressed them. Then Biancabella asked them to bring her a bucket of clear water, and bade them wash therewith her face and her maimed arms, and from these, while all were standing by, roses and violets and other flowers in great plenty fell down; whereupon they all deemed she must be some divine personage, and no mortal woman.

Now after a season it came to pass that

Biancabella felt a desire to return to the spot where first the old man had found her. But he and his wife and his daughters, seeing how great were the benefits they gathered from her presence, loaded her with endearments, and besought her very earnestly that she would on no account depart from them, bringing forward many reasons why she should not carry out her wish. But she, having resolutely made up her mind on this point, determined at all hazards to go away, promising at the same time to return to them hereafter. The old man, when he saw how firmly she was set on her departure, took her with him without any further delay back to the place where he had come upon her. And when they had reached this spot she gave directions to the old man that he should depart and leave her, bidding him also to come back there when evening should have fallen, in order that she might return with him to his house.

As soon as the old man had gone his

way the ill-fated Biancabella began to wander up and down the gloomy wood, calling loudly upon Samaritana, so that her cries and lamentations rose up even to the high heavens. But Samaritana, though she was all the while nigh to her sister, and had never for one moment abandoned her, refused as yet to answer to her call. Whereupon the wretched Biancabella, deeming that she was scattering her words upon the heedless winds, cried out, 'Alas! what further concern have I in this world, seeing that I have been bereft of my eyes and of my hands, and now at last all human help is denied to me.' And as she thus spoke there came upon her a sort of frenzy, which took away from her all hope of deliverance from her present evil case, and urged her, in despair, to lay hands upon her own life. But because there was at hand no means by which she could put an end to her miserable being, she found her way to a pool of water, which lay not far distant, in the mind there to drown herself. But when she had come to the shore of the pool, and stood thereon ready to cast herself down into the water, there sounded in her ears a voice like thunder, saying: 'Alas, alas, wretched one! keep back from self-murder, nor desire to take your own life, which you ought to preserve for some better end.' Whereupon Biancabella, alarmed by this mighty voice, felt as it were every one of her hairs standing erect on her head, but after a moment it seemed to her that she knew the voice; so, having plucked up a little courage, she said: 'Who are you who wander about these woods, proclaiming your presence to me by your kindly and pitiful words?' Then the same voice replied: 'I am Samaritana, your sister, for whom you have been calling so long and painfully.' And Biancabella, when she listened to these words, answered in a voice all broken by agonized sobs, and said: 'Alas, my sister! come to my aid, I beseech you; and if at any past time I have shown myself disregardful of your counsel, I pray you to pardon me. Indeed I have erred, and I confess my fault, but my misdeed was the fruit of my ignorance, and not of my wickedness; for be sure, if it had come from wickedness, divine justice would not have suffered me, as the author of it, so long to cumber the earth.' Samaritana, when she heard her sister's woes set forth in this pitiful story, and witnessed the cruel wrongs that had been done her, spake some comforting words, and then, having gathered divers medicinal herbs of wonderful power and virtue, she spread these over the places where Biancabella's eyes had been. Then she brought to her sister two hands, and having joined these on to the wounded wrists, at once made them whole and sound again. And when she had wrought this marvellous feat Samaritana threw off from herself the scaly skin of the serpent, and stood revealed as a maiden of lovely aspect.

The sun had already begun to veil its

glittering rays, and the evening shadows were creeping around, when the old man with anxious hasty steps returned to the wood, where he found Biancabella sitting beside a maiden wellnigh as lovely as herself. And he gazed steadily into her beauteous face, standing the while like to a man struck with wonder, and could scarcely believe it was Biancabella he looked upon. But when he was sure it was really she, he cried: 'My daughter, were you not this morning blind and bereft of your hands? How comes it that you have been thus speedily made whole again?' Biancabella answered him: 'My cure has been worked, not by anything I myself have done, but by the virtue and the kind ministering of this my dear sister who sits here beside me.' Whereupon both the sisters arose from the place where they were seated, and rejoicing greatly they went together with the old man to his house, where the wife and the three daughters gave them a most loving and hospitable welcome.

glittering rays, and the evening shadows were creeping around, when the old man with anxious hasty steps returned to the wood, where he found Biancabella sitting beside a maiden wellnigh as lovely as herself. And he gazed steadily into her beauteous face, standing the while like to a man struck with wonder, and could scarcely believe it was Biancabella he looked upon. But when he was sure

Biancabella After Her Sight And Hands Were Restored

Night the Third

THIRD FABLE

Biancabella After Her Sight And Hands Were Restored

Night the Third

THIRD FABLE

Biancabella After Her Sight And Hands Were Restored

Night the Third

THIRD FABLE

It came to pass after the lapse of many days that Samaritana and Biancabella, and the old man with his wife and his three daughters, left their cottage and betook themselves to the city of Naples, purposing to dwell there, and, when they had entered the city, they chanced to come upon a vacant space hard by the palace of the king, where they determined to make their resting-place. And when the dark night had fallen around them, Samaritana took in her hand a twig of laurel and thrice struck the earth therewith, uttering certain mystic words the while, and almost before the sound of these words had ceased there sprang up forthwith before them a palace, the most beautiful and sumptuous that ever was seen. The next morning Ferrandino the king went early to look out of the window, and when he beheld the rich and marvellous palace standing where there had been nothing the night before, he was altogether overcome with amazement, and called his wife and his stepmother to come and see it; but these were greatly disturbed in mind at the sight thereof, for a boding came upon them that some ill was about to befall them.

While Ferrandino was standing, scanning closely the palace before him, and examining it in all parts, he lifted his eyes to a certain window, and there, in the chamber inside, he beheld two ladies of a beauty more rich and dazzling than the sun. And no sooner had his eyes fallen upon them than he felt a tempest of passion rising in his heart, for he assuredly recognized in one of them some similitude of that loveliness which had once been Biancabella's. And when he asked who they were, and from what land they had come, the answer which was given him was that they were two ladies who had been exiled from their home, and that they had journeyed from Persia, with all their possessions, to take up their abode in the noble city of Naples. When he heard this, Ferrandino sent a messenger to inquire whether he would be doing them any pleasure in waiting upon them, accompanied by the ladies of his court, to pay them a visit of welcome, and to this gracious message they sent an answer, saying that it would indeed be a very precious honour to be thus visited by him, but that it would be more decorous and respectful if they, as subjects, should pay this duty to him, than that he, as lord and king, should visit them.

Hereupon Ferrandino bade them summon the queen and the other ladies of the court, and with these (although at first they refused to go, being so greatly in fear of their impending ruin) he betook himself to the palace of the two ladies, who, with all friendly signs of welcome and with modest bearing, gave him the reception due to a highly honoured guest, showing him the wide loggias, and the roomy halls, and the richly ornamented chambers, the walls of which were lined with alabaster and fine porphyry, while about them were to be seen on all sides carven figures which looked like life. And when they had exhibited to the king all parts of the sumptuous palace, the two fair young women approached Ferrandino and besought him most gracefully that he would deign to come one day with his queen and dine at their table. The king, whose heart was not hard enough to remain unaffected by all he had seen, and who was gifted moreover with a magnanimous and liberal spirit, graciously accepted the invitation. And when he had tendered his thanks to the two ladies for the noble welcome they had given him, he and the queen departed together and returned to their own palace. When the day fixed for the banquet had come, the king and the queen and the stepmother, clad in their royal robes and accompanied by some of the ladies of the court, went to do honour to the magnificent feast set out in the most sumptuous fashion. And after he had given them water to wash their hands, the seneschal bade them conduct the king and queen to a table apart, set somewhat higher, but at the same time near to the others, and having done this, he caused all the rest of the guests to seat themselves according to their rank, and in this fashion they all feasted merrily and joyfully together.

When the stately feast had come to an end and the tables had been cleared, Samaritana rose from her seat, and turning towards the king and the queen, spake thus: 'Your majesties, in order that the time may not be irksome to us, as it may if we sit here idle, let one or other of us propose something in the way of diversion which will let us pass the day pleasantly.' And when the guests heard what Samaritana said, they all agreed that she had spoken well, but yet there was found no one bold enough to make such a proposition as she had called for. Whereupon Samaritana, when she perceived they were all silent, went on: 'Since it appears that no one of this company is prepared to put forward anything, I, with your majesty's leave, will bid come hither one of our own maidens, whose singing perchance will give you no little pleasure.' And having summoned the damsel, whose name was Silveria, into the banqueting-room, Samaritana commanded her to take a lyre in her hand and to sing thereto something in honour of the king which should be worthy of their praise. And the damsel, obedient to her lady's command, took her lyre, and, having placed herself before the king, sang in a soft and pleasant voice while she touched the resounding strings with the plectrum, telling in her chant the story of Biancabella from beginning to end, but not mentioning her by name. When the whole of the story had been set forth, Samaritana again rose to her feet, and demanded of the king what would be the fitting punishment, what torture would be cruel enough for those who had put their hands to such an execrable crime. Then the stepmother, who deemed that she might perchance get a release for her misdeeds by a prompt and ready reply, did not wait for the king to give his answer, but cried out in a bold and confident tone, 'Surely to be cast into a furnace heated red hot would be but a light punishment for the offences of such a one.' Then Samaritana, with her countenance all afire with vengeance and anger, made answer to her: 'Thou thyself art the very same guilty and barbarous woman, through whose nefarious working all these cruel wrongs have been done; and thou, wicked and accursed one, hast condemned thyself to a righteous penalty out of thine own mouth.' Then Samaritana, turning towards the king with a look of joy upon her face, said to him, 'Behold! this is your Biancabella, this is the wife you loved so dearly, this is she without whom you could not live.' Then, to prove the truth of her words, Samaritana gave the word to the three daughters of the old man that they should forthwith, in the presence of the king, begin to comb Biancabella's fair and wavy hair, and scarcely had they begun when (as has been told before) there fell out of her tresses many very precious and exquisite jewels, and from her hands came forth roses exhaling the sweet scents of morning, and all manner of odoriferous flowers. And for yet greater certainty she pointed out to the king how the snow-white neck of Biancabella was encircled by a fine chain of the most delicately wrought gold, which grew naturally between the skin and the flesh, and shone out as through the clearest crystal.

When the king perceived by these manifest and convincing signs that she was indeed his own Biancabella, he began to weep for the joy he felt, and to embrace her tenderly. But before he left that place he caused to be heated hot a furnace, and into this he bade them cast the stepmother and her two daughters. Thus their repentance for their crimes came too late, and they made a miserable end

to their lives. And after this the three daughters of the old man were given honourably in marriage, and the King Ferrandino with Biancabella and Samaritana lived long and happily, and when Ferrandino died his son succeeded to his kingdom.

During the telling of Lauretta's story divers of the listeners were several times moved to tears, and, when she had brought it to an end, the Signora bade her follow the example of those who had gone before her, and set forth her enigma. Therefore she, not waiting for any further command, gave it in the following words:

A proud and cruel maid I spied,
As through the flowery meads she hied.
Behind her trailed a lengthy train,
Upreared her head in high disdain.
And swiftly on her way she took,
And sharp her touch, and eke her look.
What though her tongue moves all around,
She utters neither voice nor sound.
She is long, and thin, and wise,
He can tell her name who tries.

All the company listened attentively to the enigma which Lauretta gave to them in her sportive way, and she, when she saw there was little likelihood that anyone would find the solution thereof, spake thus: 'Dear ladies, so as not to keep you any longer in suspense, or to weary yet more your minds, which must needs be somewhat harassed on account of the pathetic story I have just told you, I will tell you the answer straightway, if such be your pleasure. The damsel I described therein is nothing else than the serpent which, when it goes through the flowery meadows, keeps its head erect and its tail trailing on the ground behind it, and frightens with its sharp eye everyone who may happen to behold it.'

As soon as Lauretta had finished her speech everyone was much astonished that the solution of the riddle had not been guessed by some one or other. And when she had resumed her seat the Signora made a sign to Alteria that she should tell them her fable, and she, having risen and made obeisance to the Signora, began it forthwith.

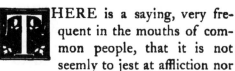

THE FOURTH FABLE.

Fortunio, on account of an injury done to him by his supposed father and mother, leaves them, and after much wandering, comes to a wood, where he finds three animals, who do him good service. Afterwards he goes to Polonia, where he gets to wife Doralice, the king's daughter, as a reward for his prowess.

THERE is a saying, very frequent in the mouths of common people, that it is not seemly to jest at affliction nor to make a mock at the truth ; forasmuch as he who keeps his eyes and ears open, and holds his tongue, is not likely to injure his fellows, and may hope himself to live in peace.

Once upon a time there lived in one of the remoter districts of Lombardy a man called Bernio, who, although he was not over well endowed with the gifts of fortune, was held to be in no way wanting with respect to good qualities of head and heart. This man took to wife a worthy and amiable woman named Alchia, who, though she chanced to be of low origin, was nevertheless of good parts and exemplary conduct, and loved her husband as dearly as any woman could. This married pair greatly desired to have children, but such a gift of God was not granted to them, peradventure for the reason that man often, in his ignorance, asks for those things which would not be to his advantage. Now, forasmuch as this desire for offspring still continued to possess them, and as fortune obstinately refused to grant their prayer, they determined at last to adopt a child whom they would nurture and treat in every way as if he were their own legitimate son. So one morning early they betook themselves to a certain spot where young children who had been cast off by their parents were often left, and, having seen there one who appeared to them more seemly and attractive than the rest, they took him home with them, and brought him up with the utmost care and good governance. Now after a time it came to pass (according to the good pleasure of Him who rules the universe and tempers and modifies everything according to His will) that Alchia became with child, and when her time of delivery was come, was brought to bed with a boy who resembled his father exactly. On this account both father and mother rejoiced exceedingly, and called their son by the name of Valentino.

The infant was well nurtured, and grew up strong and healthy and well-mannered; moreover, he loved so dearly his brother — to whom the name of Fortunio had been given — that he was inclined almost to fret himself to death whenever they chanced to be separated the one from the other. But the genius of discord, the foe of everything that is good, becoming aware of their warm and loving friendship, and being able no longer to suffer their good understanding to continue, one day interposed between them, and worked her evil will so effectively that before long the two friends began to taste her bitter fruits. Wherefore as they were sporting together one day (after the manner of boys) they grew somewhat excited over their game, and Valentino, who could not bear that Fortunio should get any advantage over him in their play, became inflamed with violent anger, and more than once called his companion a bastard and the son of a vile woman. Fortunio, when he heard these words, was much astonished, and perturbed as well, and turning to Valentino, he said to him, 'And why am I a bastard?' In reply, Valentino, muttering angrily between his teeth, repeated what he had already said, and even more. Whereupon Fortunio, greatly grieved and disturbed in mind, gave over playing and went forthwith to his so-called mother, and asked her whether he was in sooth the son of Bernio and herself. Alchia answered that he was, and, having learned that Fortunio had been insulted by Valentino, she rated the latter soundly, and declared that she would give him heavy chastisement if he should repeat his offence. But the words which Alchia had spoken roused fresh suspicion in Fortunio, and made him wellnigh certain that he was not her legitimate son; indeed, there often came upon him the desire to put her to the test, to see whether she really was his mother or not, and thus discover the truth. In the end he questioned and importuned her so closely that she acknowledged he was not born of her, but that he had been adopted and brought up in their house for the love of God and for the alleviation of the misfortune which had been sent upon herself and her husband. These words were as so many dagger-thrusts in the young man's heart, piling up one sorrow upon another, and at last his grief grew beyond endurance; but, seeing that he could not bring himself to seek refuge from his trouble by a violent death, he determined to depart from Bernio's roof, and, in wandering up and down the world, to seek a better fortune.

Alchia, when she perceived that Fortunio's desire to quit the house grew stronger every day, was greatly incensed against him, and, as she found herself powerless to dissuade him from his purpose, she heaped all sorts of curses upon him, praying that if ever he should venture upon the sea he might be engulfed in the waves and swallowed up by the sirens, as ships are often swallowed up by storms. Fortunio, driven on by a headlong access of rage, took no heed of Alchia's malediction, and, without saying any further words of farewell, either to her or to Bernio, departed, and took his way towards the east. He journeyed on, passing by marshes, by valleys, by rocks, and all kinds of wild and desert spots, and at last, one day between sext and none, he came upon a thick and densely-tangled forest, in the midst of which, by strange chance, he found a wolf and an eagle and an ant, who were engaged in a long and sharp contention over the body of a stag which they had lately captured, without being able to agree as to how the venison should be divided amongst themselves. When Fortunio came upon the three animals they were in the midst of their stubborn dispute, and not one was disposed in any way to yield to the others; but after a while they agreed that this young man, who had thus unexpectedly come amongst them, should adjudicate the matter in question, and assign to each one of them such part of the spoil as he might deem most fitting. Then, when they had assented to these preliminaries, and had promised that they would be satisfied with and observe the terms of any award he might make, even though it might seem to be unjust, Fortunio readily undertook the task, and after he had carefully considered the case, he divided the prey amongst them in the following manner. To the wolf, as to a voracious animal and one very handy with his sharp teeth, he gave, as the guerdon of his toil in the chase, all the bones of the deer and all the lean flesh. To the eagle, a rapacious fowl, but furnished with no teeth, he gave the entrails, and all the fat lying round the lean parts and the bones. To the provident and industrious ant, which had none of that strength which nature had bestowed upon the wolf and the eagle, he gave the soft brains as her share of reward for the labour she had undergone. When the three animals understood the terms of this just and carefully-considered decision, they were fully satisfied, and thanked Fortunio as well as they could for the courtesy he had shown them.

Now these three animals held — and with justice — that, of all the vices, ingratitude was the most reprehensible; so with one accord they insisted that the young man should not depart until they should have fully rewarded him for the great service he had done them. Wherefore the wolf, speaking first, said: 'My brother, I give you the power, if at any time the desire should come upon you to be a wolf instead of a man, to become one forthwith, merely by saying the words, "Would that I were a wolf!" At the same time you will be able to return to your former shape whenever you may desire.' And in like manner both the eagle and the ant endowed him with power to take upon him their form and similitude.

Then Fortunio, rejoicing greatly at the potent virtues thus given to him, and rendering to all three of the animals the warmest gratitude for their boon, took his leave and wandered far abroad, until at last he came to Polonia, a populous city of great renown, which was at that time under the rule of Odescalco, a powerful and valorous sovereign, who had but one child, a daughter called Doralice. Now the king was ambitious to find a noble mate for this princess, and it chanced that, at the time when Fortunio arrived in Polonia, he had proclaimed throughout his kingdom that a grand tournament should be held in the city, and that the Princess Doralice should be given in marriage to the man who should be the victor in the jousts. And already many dukes and marquises and other powerful nobles had come together from all parts to contend for this noble prize, and on the first day of the tournament, which had already passed, the honours of the tilting were borne off by a foul Saracen of hideous aspect and ungainly form, and with a face as black as pitch. The king's daughter, when she viewed the deformed and unseemly figure of the conqueror of the day, was overwhelmed with grief that fate should have awarded to such a one the victory in the joust, and, burying her face, which was crimson with shame, in her tender delicate hands, she wept and lamented sore, execrating her cruel and malignant destiny, and begging that death might take her rather than that she should become the wife of this misshapen barbarian. Fortunio, when he entered the city gate, noted the festal array on all sides and the great concourse of people about the streets, and when he learned the cause of all this magnificent display he was straightway possessed with an ardent desire to prove his valour by contending in the tournament, but when he came to consider that he was lacking in all the apparel needful in such honourable contests, his heart fell and heavy sorrow came over him. While he was in this doleful mood it chanced that his steps led him past the palace of the king, and raising his eyes from the ground he espied Doralice, the daughter of the king, who was leaning out of one of the windows of her apartment. She was surrounded by a group of lovely and highborn dames and maidens, but she shone out amongst them all on account of her beauty, as the radiant glorious sun shines out amidst the lesser lights of heaven.

By-and-by, when the dark night had fallen, and all the ladies of the court had retired to their apartments, Doralice, restless and sad at heart, betook herself alone to a small and exquisitely ornamented chamber and gazed once more out into the night, and there below, as luck would have it, was Fortunio. When the youth saw her standing solitary at the open window, he was so overcome by the charms of her beauty that he forthwith whispered to himself in an amorous sigh: 'Ah! wherefore am I not an eagle?' Scarcely had these words issued from his lips when he found himself transformed into an eagle, whereupon he flew at once into the window of the chamber, and, having willed to become a man again, was restored to his own shape. He went forward with a light and joyful air to greet the princess, but she, as soon as she saw him, was filled with terror and began to cry out in a loud voice, just as if she were being attacked and torn by savage dogs. The king, who happened to be in an apartment not far distant from his daughter's, heard her cries of alarm and ran immediately to seek the cause thereof, and, having heard from her that there was a young man in the room, he at once ordered it to be searched in every part. But nothing of the sort was found, because Fortunio had once more changed himself into an eagle and had flown out of the window. Hardly, however, had the father gone back to his chamber when the maiden began to cry aloud just the same as before, because, forsooth, Fortunio had once more come into her presence.

But Fortunio, when he again heard the terrified cries of the maiden, began to fear for his life, and straightway changed himself into an ant, and crept into hiding beneath the blond tresses of the lovely damsel's hair. Odescalco, hearing the loud outcries of his daughter, ran to her succour, but when he found nothing more this second time than he had found before, he was greatly incensed against her, and threatened her harshly that if she should cry out again and disturb him he would play her some trick which would not please her, and thus he left her with angry words, suspecting that what had caused her trouble was some vision of one or other of the youths who for love of her had met their deaths in the tournament. Fortunio listened attentively to what the king said to his daughter, and, as soon as he had left the apartment, once more put off the shape of an ant and stood revealed in his own form. Doralice, who in the meanwhile had gone to bed, was so terror-stricken when she saw him that she tried to spring from her couch and to give the alarm, but she was not able to do this, because Fortunio placed one of his hands on her lips, and thus spake: 'Signora, fear not that I have come here to despoil you of your honour, or to steal aught that belongs to you. I am come rather to succour you to the best of my power, and to proclaim myself your most humble servant. If you cry out, one or other of two misfortunes will befall us, either your honour and fair name will be tarnished, or you will be the cause of your death and of my own. Therefore, dear lady of my heart, take care lest at the same time you cast a stain upon your reputation and imperil the lives of us both.'

While Fortunio was thus speaking, Doralice was weeping bitterly, her presence of mind being completely overthrown by this unexpected declaration on his part, and the young man, when he perceived how powerfully agitated she was, went on addressing her in words gentle and persuasive enough to have melted the heart of a stone. At last, conquered by his words and tender manner, she softened towards him, and consented to let him make his peace with her. And after a little, when she saw how handsome the youth was in face, and how strong and well knit in body and limb, she fell a-thinking about the ugliness and deformity of the Saracen, who, as the conqueror in the jousts, must before long be the master of her person. While these thoughts were passing through her mind the young man said to her: 'Dear lady, if I had the fitting equipment, how willingly would I enter the jousts to tilt on your behalf, and my heart tells me that, were I to contend, I should surely conquer.' Whereupon the damsel in reply said: 'If this, indeed, were to come to pass, if you should prove victorious in the lists, I would give myself to you alone.' And when she saw what a well-disposed youth he was, and how ardent in her cause, she brought forth a great quantity of gems and a heavy purse of gold, and bade him take them. Fortunio accepted them with his heart full of joy, and inquired of her what garb she wished him to wear in the lists to-morrow. And she bade him array himself in white satin, and in this matter he did as she commanded him.

On the following day Fortunio, encased in polished armour, over which he wore a surcoat of white satin richly embroidered with the finest gold, and studded with jewels most delicately carven, rode into the piazza unknown to anybody there present. He was mounted on a powerful and fiery charger, which was caparisoned and decked in the same colours as its rider. The crowd, which had already come together to witness the grand spectacle of the tournament, no sooner caught sight of the gallant unknown champion, with lance in hand all ready for the fray, than every person was lost in wonderment at so brave a sight, and each one, gazing fixedly at Fortunio, and astonished at his grace, began to inquire of his neighbour: 'Ah! who can this knight be who rides so gallantly and splendidly arrayed into the lists? Know you not what is his name?' In the meantime Fortunio, having entered the lists, called upon some rival to advance, and for the first course the Saracen presented himself, whereupon the two champions, keeping low the points of their trusty lances, rushed one upon the other like two lions loosened from their bonds, and so shrewd was the stroke dealt by Fortunio upon the head of the Saracen, that the latter was driven right over the crupper of his horse, and fell dead upon the bare earth, mangled and broken up as a fragile glass is broken when it is thrown against a wall. And Fortunio ran his course just as victoriously in encountering every other champion who ventured to oppose him in the lists. The damsel, when she saw how the fortune of the day was going, was greatly rejoiced, and kept her eyes steadily fixed on Fortunio in deepest admiration, and, thanking God in her heart for having thus graciously delivered her from the bondage of the Saracen, prayed to Him that this brave youth might be the final victor.

When the night had come they bade Doralice come to supper with the rest of the court; but to this bidding she made demur, and commanded them bring her certain rich viands and delicate wines to her chamber, feigning that she had not yet any desire for food, but would eat, perchance, later on if any appetite should come upon her. Then, having locked herself in her chamber and opened the window thereof, she watched with ardent desire for the coming of her lover, and when he had gained admittance to the chamber by the same means as he had used the previous day, they supped joyfully together. Then Fortunio demanded of her in what fashion she would that he should array himself for the morrow, and she made answer that he must bear a badge of green satin all embroidered with the finest thread of silver and gold, and that his horse should be caparisoned in like manner. On the following morning Fortunio appeared, attired as Doralice had directed, and, having duly presented himself in the piazza at the appointed time, he entered the lists and proved himself again as valiant a champion as he had proved to be on the day before. So great was the admiration of the people of his prowess, that the shout went up with one voice that he had worthily won the gracious princess for his bride.

On the evening of that day the princess, full of merriment and happiness and joyous expectations, made the same pretext for absenting herself from supper as she had made the day before, and, having locked the door of her chamber, awaited there the coming of her lover, and supped pleasantly with him. And when he asked her once more with what vestments he should clothe himself on the following day, she answered that she wished him to wear a surcoat of crimson satin, all worked and embroidered with gold and pearls, and to see that the trappings of his horse were made in the same fashion; adding that she herself would, on the morrow, be clad in similar wise. 'Lady,' replied Fortunio, 'if by any chance I should tarry somewhat in making my entry into the lists, be not astonished, for I shall not be late without good cause.'

When the morning of the third day had come, the spectators awaited the issue of the momentous strife with the most earnest expectation, but, on account of the inexhaustible valour of the gallant unknown champion, there was no opponent found who dared to enter the lists against him, and he himself for some hidden reason did not appear. After a time the spectators began to grow impatient at his non-appearance, and injurious words were dropped. Even Doralice herself was assailed by suspicions as to his worth, although she had been warned by Fortunio himself that probably his coming would be delayed: so, overcome by this hidden trouble of hers —concerning which no one else knew anything—she wellnigh swooned with grief. At last, when it was told to her that the unknown knight was advancing into the piazza, her failing senses began to revive. Fortunio was clad in a rich and sumptuous dress, and the trappings of his horse were of the finest cloth of gold, all embroidered with shining rubies and emeralds and sapphires and great pearls. When the people saw these they affirmed that the price of them would be equal to a great kingdom, and when Fortunio came into the piazza, every one cried out in a loud voice: 'Long live the unknown knight!' and after this they all applauded vigorously and clapped their hands. Then the jousting began, and Fortunio once more carried himself so valiantly that he bore to earth all those who dared to oppose him, and in the end was hailed as the victor in the tournament. And when he had dismounted from his noble horse, the chief magnates and the wealthy citizens of the town bore him aloft on their shoulders, and to the sound of trumpets and all other kinds of musical instruments, and with loud shouts which went up to the heavens, they carried him into the presence of the king. When they had taken off his helmet and his shining armour the king perceived what a seemly graceful youth he was, and, having called his daughter into his presence, he betrothed them forthwith, and celebrated the nuptials with the greatest pomp, keeping open table at the court for the space of a month.

After Fortunio had lived for a certain space of time in loving dalliance with his fair wife, he was seized one day with the thought that he was playing the part of an unworthy sluggard in thus passing the days in indolence, merely counting the hours as they sped by, after the manner of foolish folk, and of those who consider not the duties of a man. Wherefore he made up his mind to go afield into certain regions, where there might be found due scope and recognition for his valour and enterprise; so, having got ready a galley and taken a large treasure which his father-in-law had given him, he embarked after taking leave of his wife and of King Odescalco. He sailed away, wafted on by gentle and favourable breezes, until he came into the Atlantic Ocean, but before he had gone more than ten miles thereon, there arose from the waves the most beautiful Siren that ever was seen, and singing softly, she began to swim towards the ship. Fortunio, who was reclining by the side of the galley, bent his head low down over the water to listen to her song, and straightway fell asleep, and, while he thus slept, the Siren drew him gently from where he lay, and, bearing him in her arms, sank with him headlong into the depths of the sea. The mariners, after having vainly essayed to save him, broke out into loud lamentations over his sad fate, and, weeping and mourning, they decked the galley with black ensigns of grief, and returned to the unfortunate Odescalco to tell him of the terrible mischance which had befallen them during their voyage. The king and Doralice, when the sad news was brought to them, were overwhelmed with the deepest grief —as indeed was everyone else in the city—and all put on garments of mourning black.

Now at the time of Fortunio's departure Doralice was with child, and when the season of her delivery had come she gave birth to a beautiful boy, who was delicately and carefully nurtured until he came to be two years of age. At this time the sad and despairing Doralice, who had always brooded over her unhappy fate in losing the company of her beloved husband, began to abandon all hope of ever seeing him again; so she, like a brave and great-souled woman, resolved to put her fortune to the test and go to seek for him upon the deep, even though the king her father should not consent to let her depart. So she caused to be set in order for her voyage an armed galley, well fitted for such a purpose, and she took with her three apples, each one a masterpiece of handicraft, of which one was fashioned out of golden bronze, another of silver, and the last of the finest gold. Then, having taken leave of her father the king, she embarked with her child on board the galley, and sailed away before a prosperous wind into the open sea.

After the sad and woe-stricken lady had sailed a certain time over the calm sea, she bade the sailors steer the ship forthwith towards the spot where her husband had been carried off by the Siren, and this command they immediately obeyed. And when the vessel had been brought to the aforesaid spot, the child began to cry fretfully, and would in no wise be pacified by his mother's endearments; so she gave him the apple which was made of golden bronze to appease him. While the child was thus sporting with the apple, he was espied by the Siren, who, having come near to the galley and lifted her head a little space out of the foaming waves, thus spake to Doralice: 'Lady, give me that apple, for I desire greatly to have it.' But the princess answered her that this thing could not be done, inasmuch as the apple was her child's plaything. 'If you will consent to give it to me,' the Siren went on, 'I will show you the husband you have lost as far as his breast.' Doralice, when she heard these words, at once took the apple from the child and handed it courteously to the Siren, for she longed above all things else to get sight of her beloved husband.

The Siren was faithful to her promise, and after a little time brought Fortunio to the surface of the sea and showed him as far as the breast to Doralice, as a reward for the gift of the apple, and then plunged with him once more into the depths of the ocean, and disappeared from sight.

Doralice, who had naturally feasted her eyes upon the form of her husband what time he was above the water, only felt the desire to see him once more grow stronger after he was gone under again, and, not knowing what to do or to say, she sought comfort in the caresses of her child, and when the little one began to cry once more, the mother gave to it the silver apple to soothe its fancy. Again the Siren was on the watch and espied the silver apple in the child's hand, and having raised her head above the waves, begged Doralice to give her the apple, but the latter, shrugging her shoulders, said that the apple served to divert the child, and could not be spared. Whereupon the Siren said: 'If only you will give me this apple, which is far more beautiful than the other, I promise I will show you your husband as far as his knees.' Poor Doralice, who was now consumed with desire to see her beloved husband again, put aside the satisfaction of the child's fancy, and, having taken away from him the silver apple, handed it eagerly to the Siren, who, after she had once more brought Fortunio to the surface and exhibited him to Doralice as far as his knees (according to her promise), plunged again beneath the waves.

For a while the princess sat brooding in silent grief and suspense, trying in vain to hit upon some plan by which she might rescue her husband from his piteous fate, and at last she caught up her child in her arms and tried to comfort herself with him and to still his weeping. The child, mindful of the fair apple he had been playing with, continued to cry; so the mother, to appease him, gave him at last the apple of fine gold. When the covetous Siren, who was still watching the galley, saw this apple, and perceived that it was much fairer than either of the others, she at once demanded it as a gift from Doralice, and she begged so long and persistently, and at last made a promise to the princess that, in return for the gift of this apple, she would bring Fortunio once more into the light, and show him from head to foot; so Doralice took the apple from the boy, in spite of his chiding, and gave it to the Siren. Whereupon the latter, in order to carry out her promise, came quite close to the galley, bearing Fortunio upon her back, and having raised herself somewhat above the surface of the water, showed the person of Fortunio from head to foot. Now, as soon as Fortunio felt that he was quite clear of the water, and resting free upon the back of the Siren, he was filled with great joy in his heart, and, without hesitating for a moment, he cried out, 'Ah! would that I were an eagle,' and scarcely had he ceased speaking when he was forthwith transformed into an eagle, and, having poised himself for flight, he flew high above the sail yards of the galley, from whence — all the shipmen looking on the while in wonder — he descended into the ship and returned to his proper shape, and kissed and embraced his wife and his child and all the sailors on the galley.

Then, all of them rejoicing at the rescue of Fortunio, they sailed back to

Fortunio Disguised As An Eagle
Escapes From The Siren

Fortunio Disguised As An Eagle Escapes From The Siren

Night the Third

FOURTH FABLE

Fortunio Disguised As An Eagle
Escapes From The Siren

Night the Third

FOURTH FABLE

Fortunio Disguised As An Eagle Escapes From The Siren

Night the Third

FOURTH FABLE

King Odescalco's kingdom, and as soon as they entered the port they began to play upon the trumpets and tabors and drums and all the other musical instruments they had with them, so that the king, when he heard the sound of these, was much astonished, and in the greatest suspense waited to learn what might be the meaning thereof. And before very long time had elapsed the herald came before him, and announced to the king how his dear daughter, having rescued her husband from the Siren, had come back. When they were disembarked from the galley, they all repaired to the royal palace, where their return was celebrated by sumptuous banquets and rejoicings. But after some days had passed, Fortunio betook himself for a while to his old home, and there, after having transformed himself into a wolf, he devoured Alchia, his adoptive mother, and Valentino her son, in revenge for the injuries they had worked him. Then, after he had returned to his rightful shape, he mounted his horse and rode back to his father-in-law's kingdom, where, with Doralice his dear wife, he lived in peace for many years to the great delight of both of them.

As soon as Alteria had brought to an end her long and interesting story the Signora bade her at once to set forth her enigma, and she, smiling pleasantly, obeyed the command.

Far from this our land doth dwell
One who by turns is fair or fell;
Springing from a twofold root,
One part woman, one part brute.
Now like beauty's fairest jewel,
Now a monster fierce and cruel.
Sweetest song on vocal breath,
To lead men down to shameful death.

Alteria's most fitting and noteworthy enigma was answered in divers fashion by the listeners, some giving one interpretation of it and some another, but not one of them came upon its exact meaning. Therefore, when the fair Alteria saw there was little chance of anyone finding the true answer, she said: "Ladies and gentlemen, the real subject of my enigma is the fascinating Siren who is fabled to dwell in the deep sea. She is very fair to look upon, for her head and breast and body and arms are those of a beautiful damsel, but all the rest of her form is scaly like a fish, and in her nature she is cunning and cruel. She sings so sweetly that the mariners, when they hear her song, are soothed to slumber, and while they sleep she drowns them in the sea." When the listeners heard this clever and subtle solution given by Alteria, they praised it warmly with one accord, declaring the while that it was most ingenious. And she, smiling with pleasure and gratitude, rose from her chair and thanked them for their kindness in thus lending their attention to her story. As soon as she had taken her seat, the Signora made a sign to Eritrea to follow in the due order with her story, and she, blushing like a morning rose, began it in these words.

THE FIFTH FABLE.

Isotta, the wife of Lucaferro Albani of Bergamo, devises how she may trick Travaglino the cowherd of her brother Emilliano and thereby show him to be a liar, but she loses her husband's farm and returns home worsted in her attempt, and bringing with her a bull's head with gilded horns.

SO great is the strength of truth, our infallible guide, that, according to the testimony of Holy Writ, it would be easier for heaven and earth to pass away than for truth to fail. And so far-reaching a charter has truth, as is written by all the wise men of the world, that she is ever the victor of time, and time never victor over her. Like as oil, if it be poured in a vessel together with water, will always rise to the top, so will truth always assert herself over falsehood. Wherefore on this account let no one be amazed over this prologue of mine, seeing that

I have set it down, moved thereto by the malignity of a wicked woman, who, deeming that she might, by the means of her false allurements, lead on a young fellow to tell a lie, only induced him to speak the plain truth to her own confusion, the which, wicked woman as she was, she well merited. All this I propose to set before you in this story of mine, which I hope, both as to time and place, will prove more profitable than hurtful to all of you.

I will first tell my worthy hearers that in Bergamo, an ancient city of Lombardy, there lived not a great time ago a man of wealth and standing whose name was Pietromaria di Albini. To this man were born two sons, of whom one was called Emilliano, and the other Lucaferro. He possessed also two farms in a township not far removed, one of them known by the name of Ghorem, and the other by that of Pedrench. The two brothers, that is to say, Emilliano and Lucaferro, divided the farms between them by lot after the death of Pietromaria their father, and Pedrench fell to the share of Emilliano, and Ghorem to Lucaferro. Now Emilliano owned a very fine flock of sheep, and a herd of lusty young bullocks, and likewise a second herd of productive cows, and over the whole of these cattle one Travaglino had charge as herdsman, a man of the most approved truth and loyalty, who, however dear he held his life, would not have told a lie to save it, and who, moreover, as a herdsman had not his equal in all the world. With his herd of cows, Travaglino kept several very fine bulls, amongst which there was one especially beautiful in appearance, and so great a favourite was this bull with Emilliano that he caused its horns to be gilded over with the finest gold. And as often as Travaglino might go to Bergamo after his affairs, Emilliano would never fail to question him as to the welfare of his favourite bull with the gilded horns.

It happened one day that while Emilliano was entertaining and holding converse with his brother Lucaferro and with divers other of his friends, Travaglino came anigh the company and made a sign to Emilliano his master that he wanted to speak with him. Whereupon the latter forthwith withdrew from the presence of his brother and his friends, and having gone apart with Travaglino, held him there some long time in conversation. And after this it would happen full often that Emilliano would do the like, and leave his friends and family who might be about him, and betake himself aside to confer with his herdsman; so that at last Lucaferro, his brother, lost patience at such doings, and could endure them no longer. On one occasion, therefore, hot with wrath and indignation, he spake to Emilliano in these words: 'Emilliano, I am astonished beyond measure at your behaviour, that you make more account of this rascally cowherd of yours than you make of your own brother and of your many trusted friends; because, forsooth, not once, but a thousand times, if

I may so express myself, you have gone away from us when we were together in the piazza, or over our games, as if we had been so many beasts only fit to be driven to the shambles, to go and foregather with this lubberly ruffian of a Travaglino, your hireling, and to have long converse with him, making believe that the affairs you had to discuss with him were of the highest importance, while in fact nothing you talked about mattered a single straw.' To this Emilliano made answer: 'Lucaferro, my good brother, there is surely no need for you to fly into so hot a passion with me, while you heap all these injurious words upon poor Travaglino, who, after all, is a very worthy young fellow, and one on whom I set great store, both on account of his efficiency in his calling and for his staunch loyalty towards myself; moreover, he has yet another and special good quality, inasmuch as he would not, to gain all the wealth there is in the world, speak a word which was not the truth. And furthermore he has many other excellent traits on account of which I hold him in high esteem; therefore there is no reason why you should be astonished at my fondness for him, or that I should treat him kindly.'

This answer given by Emilliano only served to stir yet deeper his brother's bile, and they straightway began to bandy angry words from one to the other, so that they narrowly escaped coming to blows. In the end Lucaferro, on account of the high commendation pronounced by Emilliano over Travaglino's good qualities — the which is written above — thus spake: 'You speak loud enough to-day of the efficiency, and the good faith, and the truthfulness of this cowherd of yours, but I tell you that he is the most bungling, the most disloyal loon in the world, as well as the biggest liar that nature ever made. And moreover I will pledge myself to bring all this to your notice, and to let you hear him tell a falsehood before your very face.' After they had spent much time in wrangling, they ended by wagering their respective farms over the question, settling the affair in this fashion, namely, that if Travaglino should be proved to be a liar, the farm of Emilliano should pass to Lucaferro; but if on the other hand, he should be found truthful, Emilliano should become the owner of Lucaferro's. And over this matter, having called in a notary, they caused to be drawn up a legal instrument ratified by all the forms which are required in such cases.

After the brothers had parted one from the other, and after their wrath and indignation had gone down somewhat, Lucaferro began to be sore repentant of the wager he had made, and of the legal instrument he had requested to be enacted under the seal of the notary. Wherefore he found himself mightily troubled over the affair, and haunted by the fear lest at the end of it he might find himself deprived of his farm, out of which alone he had to find sustenance for himself and for his family. One day, when he was in his house, his wife, whose name was Isotta, remarked that he was in a very melancholy mood, and not knowing the reason thereof, she said to him: 'Heigho, my good husband! what can be the matter with you that you are so dismal and woebegone?' And Lucaferro made answer to her: 'Wife, hold your tongue, for goodness sake, and do not heap any fresh trouble upon me in addition to what I am plagued with already.' Whereupon Isotta began to be very curious to know what this trouble might be, and she plied her husband so skilfully with questions that in the end he told her everything. Then she said to him, with her face all radiant with joy and satisfaction: 'And is it really on account of this apprehension that you have got into such a taking of fear and agitation? Keep up a good heart, for you will see that I have wit enough in me to make this lout Travaglino tell to his master's face, not one lie, but a thousand.' And Lucaferro, when he heard these words, was much comforted.

to lay out h
So, having d
ion calculate
and daintly
her way by h
went to Ped
the farm of E
into the farm
Travaglino, wl
and curds of
him, saying: '
low, you see I
visit, to take a
eat some of yo
I am very glad
Travaglino rep
her sit down, h
table, and to pla
ewe's milk and
to do the lady
while the youth

alone and very fair to look upon, was somewhat taken aback, forasmuch as it was in no way her wont thus to visit him, and could hardly persuade himself that she could be in truth Isotta, the wife of his master's brother. However, because he had often before seen her, he did his best to please her and to pay her such honour as would have been due to any lady, let her be whosoever she might.

After the meal was despatched and the table cleared, Isotta, observing that Travaglino was about to go to his cheese-making and to strain his whey, said to him: 'Travaglino, my good fellow, I would fain lend you a hand in making your cheese.' And he answered her: 'Yes, if it would please you, signora.' Then, without saying another word, she tucked up her sleeves as far as her elbows, thus laying bare her fair, wanton, well-rounded arms, which shone out as white as snow, and set to work with a will to help Travaglino to make his cheese, letting him now and again get a peep at her swelling bosom, where he might also see her breasts, which seemed as round and firm as two fair globes. And, besides this, she artfully brought her own rosy cheek mighty close to Travaglino's face, so that occasionally one touched the other. Now, Travaglino, notwithstanding that he was only a simple countryman and a cowherd, was by no means wanting in wit, and, although he understood well enough from the looks and the demeanour of the lady that she was fired by lecherous passion, he did nothing more in the way of a return than beguile her by ordinary speech and glances, making believe the while to wot nothing of making love. But Isotta, who began to persuade herself that the young man was all on fire with love for her, felt herself straightway so mightily inflamed with amorous desire toward him that she could with difficulty hold herself within bounds. Although Travaglino perceived well enough what was

Isotta And Travaglino

Night the Third

FIFTH FABLE

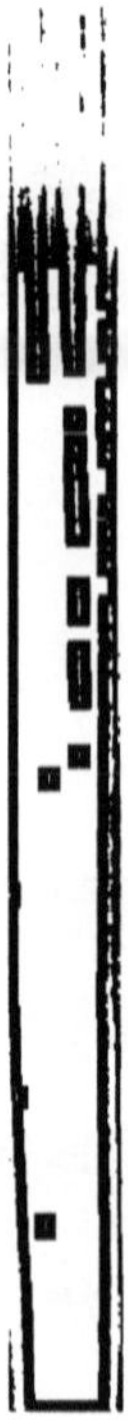

Isotta And Travaglino

Night the Third

FIFTH FABLE

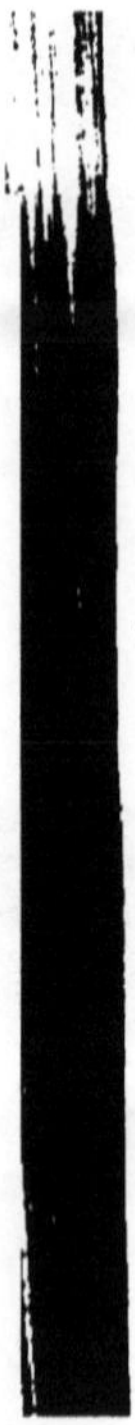

Isotta And Travaglino

Night the Third

FIFTH FABLE

the drift of the lady's lascivious wishes, he did not dare to say a word to her thereanent, fearing lest he might unduly trouble her and perhaps give offence. Wherefore the lovesick dame, by way of making an end of Travaglino's bashful dallying, said to him: 'Travaglino, what is the reason that you stand there so mum and thoughtful, and do not venture to say a word to me? Peradventure there has come into your head the wish to ask some favour of me. Take good care and do not keep your desire a secret, whatever it may be, since by so doing you will work an injury to yourself, and not me, seeing that I am completely at your pleasure and wish.' Travaglino, when he heard these words, put on a more sprightly manner and made a pretence of being greatly wishful to enjoy her. The besotted dame, when she saw that the young man at last gave signs of being moved to amorous intent, determined that the time had come to set about the business on which she was bent, so she spake to him thus: 'Travaglino, I am going to ask you to do me a great favour, and, if you should be churlish enough to refuse to grant it, I tell you plainly that it will look as if you held very light the love I bear you; moreover, your refusal will perchance be the cause of my ruin, or even of my death.'

To this speech Travaglino answered: 'Signora, for the love I have for you I am ready to devote my life and all I possess in the world to your service, and if it should chance that you demand of me to carry out some enterprise of great difficulty, nevertheless, on account of my own love and of the love which you have shown for me, I will easily accomplish it.' Then Isotta, taking courage from these words of Travaglino, said: 'If indeed you are my friend, as I well believe you to be, I shall know full soon.' 'Lay what command on me you will, signora,' replied Travaglino, 'and you will see clearly enough whether I am your friend or not.' 'All that I want of you, said Isotta, 'is the head of that bull of yours which has his horns gilded. Give me this, and you may do with me what you please.' Travaglino, when he heard this request, was well-nigh overcome with amazement; but, inflamed by the pricks of fleshly desire, and by the allurements of the lustful woman before him, he made answer to her: 'Signora, can it be that this is all you want of me? You shall have, not only the head of the bull, but the body as well; nay, I will hand over my own self into your keeping.' And after he had thus spoken, Travaglino plucked up heart and folded the lady in his arms, and they together took part in the sweetest delights of love. When this was done, Travaglino cut off the bull's head, and, having put it in a sack, handed it over to Isotta, who, well satisfied that she had accomplished her purpose and got much pleasure and delight besides, made her way back to her house, bearing with her more horns than farms in her sack.

Now Travaglino, as soon as the lady had taken her departure, began to feel somewhat troubled in mind and to cast about for some excuse which he might bring forward to his master when he should be called upon to account for the death of the bull with the gilded horns, which was so greatly beloved by Emilliano. While the wretched Travaglino was held by these torments of his mind, knowing neither what to say or to do, it came into his head at last to take a branch of one of the pruned trees which grew about, and to dress this up with some of his own poor garments, and to make believe that it was Emilliano. Then, standing before this scarecrow, he proposed to make trial of what he should do and say when he should be brought face to face with his master. Wherefore, after he had set up the tree branch thus bedizened in a chamber of the house with his own cap on its head and with certain of his garments upon its back, Travaglino went out from the chamber for a short space of time, and then came back and entered, saluting the branch as he went in, and saying, 'Good day, my master!' and then, making answer out of his own mouth, he replied, 'I am glad to see you, Travaglino. How do you find yourself, and how are things going on at the farm? It is a long time since I have seen anything of you.' 'I am very well,' replied Travaglino, 'but I have been so busy of late that I have not been able to find time to come and see you.' 'How did you leave the bull with the gilded horns?' asked Emilliano, and then Travaglino made as if he would answer: 'Master, I have to tell you that your favourite bull has been eaten of wolves while he was straying in the woods.' 'Then where are his skin and his gilded horns?' Emilliano inquired. And when he had come to this point poor Travaglino could not hit upon any answer he could possibly give; so, wellnigh overcome with grief, he left the chamber. After a little he came in again and recom-

do

self

of that

was such a pet with his master? How will he clear himself of such a trouble as this without telling a lie or two? See, here is the head of the bull, which I have brought back with me to use as a testimony against him when he shall begin with his false tales.' But the dame said not a word to her husband as to how she had made for his own benefit two fine horns, bigger than those of a hart royal. Lucaferro, when he saw the bull's head, was overjoyed and could hardly contain himself for glee, making sure that he would now win his wager, but the issue of the affair fell out in mighty different fashion, as you will learn later on.

Travaglino, after he had essayed divers bouts of questions and answers with his scarecrow man, discoursing just as if he were in conversation with the master himself, and finding in the end that they none of them would serve the end he had in view, made up his mind without further ado to go and seek his master forthwith, no matter what might happen. Wherefore, having set forth towards Bergamo, he presented himself before his master, to whom he gave a hearty salute. Emilliano, after he had greeted his herdsman in return, said to him, 'And what business has been taking up all your time and thoughts of late, Travaglino, that you have let so many days pass without coming here or without letting us have any news of you?' Travaglino replied, 'Master, the many jobs I have had in hand have kept me fully occupied.' Then said Emilliano, 'And how goes on my bull with the gilded horns?'

When he heard these words, poor Travaglino was overcome with the direst confusion, and his face flushed with shame as red as a burning furnace, and he was fain to find some excuse for his fault and to hide the truth. But in the end the fear of saying aught which might sully his honour stood him in good stead, and made him take heart of grace and tell his master the whole story from beginning to end: how Isotta had beguiled him, and how his dealings with her had ensued in the death of the bull. Emilliano was amazed beyond measure as he listened to this story, which, however great his fault might have been, at least proved Travaglino to be a truthful fellow and one of good character. So in the end Emilliano won the wager with regard to the farm, and Lucaferro gained nothing but a pair of horns for his own head, while his good-for-nothing wife Isotta, in trying to dupe another, was finely duped herself, and got nothing but shame for her trouble.

When this instructive fable was finished, every one of the worthy company of listeners was loud in blame of the dissolute Isotta, and equally loud in commendation of Travaglino, holding up to ridicule the silly loose-minded woman, who had in such vile manner given herself away to a herdsman, of which ill-doing the real cause was her innate and pestilential avarice. And seeing that Eritrea had not as yet propounded her enigma, the Signora, glancing at her, made a sign that she must not interrupt the procedure they had followed so far. Whereupon Eritrea, without any farther delay, gave her enigma:

I saw one day in fine spring weather,
A head and a breech full close together.
Another breech I likewise found
Squatting at ease upon the ground.
And one, as strong as any mule,
Stood quiet, subject to the rule
Of two, who in the head shone bright,
And looked with pleasure on the sight.
Meantime the head pressed closer still,
And ten there were who worked with will,
With dexterous grasp, now up, now down.
No prettier sight in all the town.

Though the ladies made merry enough over the fable, they held the enigma to be no less of a jest. And, because there was not one of them who seemed likely to be able to solve it, Eritrea spake as follows: "My enigma, ladies and gentlemen, is intended to describe one who sits down under a cow and sets to work to milk her. And for the same reason he who milks the cow must keep his head close to the cow's breech, and the milker, for his good convenience, sits with his breech on the ground. She is very patient, and is kept in restraint by one, namely, he who milks her, and is watched by two eyes, and is stroked by two hands and the ten fingers, which draw from her the milk." This very clever enigma pleased them all mightily, as well as the interpretation thereof; but, seeing that every star had now disappeared from the heaven, save only a certain one which still shone in the whitening dawn, the Signora gave order that every one of the company should depart whithersoever he would, and take rest until the coming evening, commanding at the same time that each one should duly appear again at the appointed place under pain of her displeasure.

The End of the Third Night.

Contents.

Volume One.

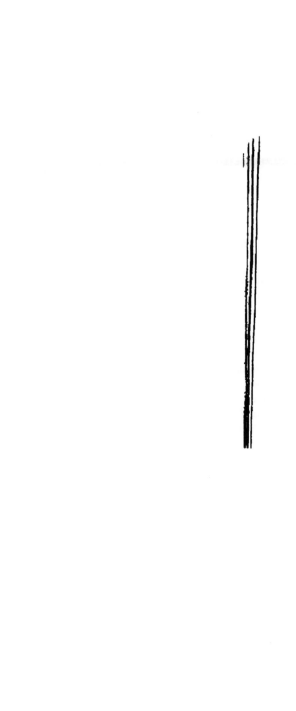

List of Illustrations.

VOLUME ONE.

Here endeth the First Volume.

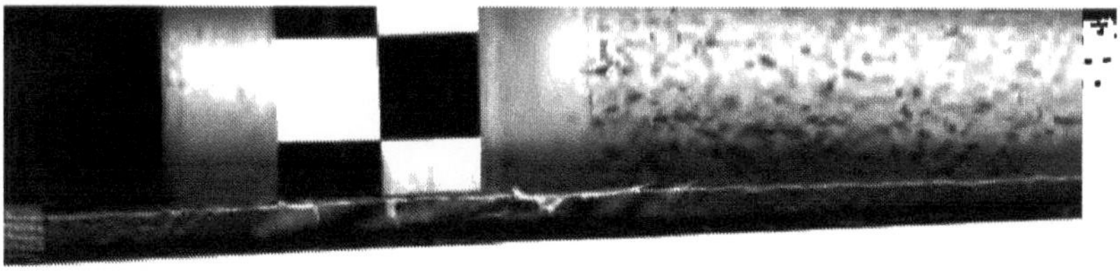

Milton Keynes UK
Ingram Content Group UK Ltd.
UKHW022014160823
426999UK00004B/61

9 781015 672239